Ian Walker is 34 years old, and lives in South London. He has been a chef for 17 years, working in many of the capital's top restaurants, and he has a passion for food, travel and adventure.

He currently works as a food consultant and has a stall at Marylebone Farmers' market. He is an experienced traveller, having covered much of Africa, Asia, Australasia and Europe.

Sourcing locally produced food is Ian's main food passion, and one that he is keen to promote at all times.

ian walker

thirty miles

a local journey in food

Matador
9 De Montfort Mews
Leicester LE1 7FW, UK
Tel: (+44) 116 255 9311 / 9312
Email: books@troubador.co.uk
Web: www.troubador.co.uk/matador

ISBN 1 905237 64 2

Typeset in 11pt Gill Sans by Troubador Publishing Ltd, Leicester, UK
Printed in the UK by The Cromwell Press Ltd, Trowbridge, Wilts, UK

Matador is an imprint of Troubador Publishing Ltd

to the guardians of the land and sea
to all believers in the local way
forward ever, backward never

Contents

Introduction

In August 2004, I was invited for a break to the tiny village of Aberdaron, situated on the tip of the Llyn Peninsula in North Wales. Having only previously ventured as far as the beautiful mountains of Snowdonia, I'll admit to not knowing that area of Wales at all.

I stayed in a cottage, perched high up on the cliffs facing out to sea, just a short walk to the village, affording you views of the ocean, and a gentle stroll affording you views of the sweeping expanse of Aberdaron Bay. In August this place is incredibly popular; the beach busy, inns full and the old teashop does a roaring trade.

I had been warned that, being a chef, I might find the place a little wanting in culinary inspiration. Indeed, a relative of the family who owned the cottage had taken a great deal of persuasion to visit because of what he termed the lack of good food. On first reflection, his comments are not without merit. After all, there is only a small supermarket, tiny baker's, newsagent, a couple of pubs, two small teashops and a handful of tourist shops. However, I couldn't accept that the surrounding area, which included world class grazing land, an ocean stocked with fish and people with a passion for food, could not produce high quality fayre.

It was this that sowed the seed of my challenge. Where was the good food around here? I spent the week writing recipes based on what was available... the fish from locals, the vegetables from a smallholding on the other side of the village, blackberries from the hedgerow, and even duck from the baker! When I came to the end of the week, I realised that I had only scratched the surface, so I moved back for three months to explore a little further afield. The people I met all inspired me to continue and *Thirty Miles* was born.

My aim was to put a point in the map, and then source all the food I could find from within a thirty mile radius, as the crow flies. The nearest large town to me was Pwllheli, which gave me a natural point from which to begin.

One of the main driving forces for me is the need to appreciate where our food comes from – to know what happens to it prior to hitting our plates, and to have total confidence in the producers.

This book is about the individuals I met on my travels, and is dedicated to them all. Without their spirit, this book wouldn't have been written. It highlights some of the issues we face in this country with regards to food, and gives an insight into the daily lives of smaller producers... their struggles, triumphs and vision for the future.

Make no mistake, I had a lot of fun on this trip, and met some memorable people. However, it did emphasise the problems facing smaller producers, particularly the continued 'steamroller' that is the supermarket. Buying locally has many benefits, and some areas are very good at promoting this. Farmers' markets are popping up all the time, but they are a tiny percentage of the overall market, and need our continued support.

Many of the recipes in this book are very simple, though a few will challenge. All the main ingredients were sourced within the thirty mile radius, with the store cupboard items being the only exceptions. When experimenting with this book, I urge you to search out the local food outlets near you, including butchers, fishmongers, greengrocers, farm shops and bakers. Pay special attention to the signs at the side of the road, as you could be in for a real treat. Understanding where the food on your plate comes from is the minimum you should require.

Good cooking needs great passion, patience and respect for the food you are about to create, and respecting the people who produce it has never been more vital.

I J Walker

Acknowledgements

I would like to thank the following:

Jill and Mike Langley, Steve Harrison, Sion Jenkins, Mary and Gareth White, Fiona and Brian Thomas, Michael and Rosalind Hooton, Joyce and Emlyn, Anne Parry, Elwyn (Ryhd-d-Cladfy), Shaun Krijjen, Rowena Mansfield, David at Deri Mon, William Jones, Bini Jones, Peter Haywood, Lewis Jones, Margaret Davies, Gwyn Thomas, Ifan Jones, Jackie at Glasfryn Park. Without you this book wouldn't exist and you inspired me at all times to complete it. There are many people whose name I never knew but if you helped me in anyway, a big thanks. Belinda Bush at Ecologist magazine, Liz Wright at Friends of the Earth, Jayne Roberts at Mentor Mon, Richard at Rare Breeds Survival Trust, Melissa Kidd at Soil Association, Andrew James at Welsh Black Beef Society. Sally Kemmis-Betty for the kind use of the cottage in Aberdaron. Rebecca Walker, for her advice and direct approach. Andrew Sullivan for designing the front cover and Danielle St Pierre for the illustrations. All my friends (just for being my mates), all players of musical instruments and lastly my Mum and Dad for putting up with my wanderings over the years.

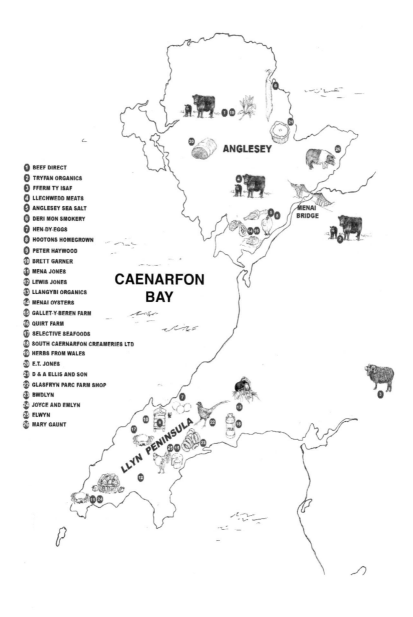

ANGLESEY

CAENARFON
BAY

MENAI
BRIDGE

LLYN PENINSULA

1. BEEF DIRECT
2. TRYFAN ORGANICS
3. FFERM TY ISAF
4. LLECHWEDD MEATS
5. ANGLESEY SEA SALT
6. DERI MON SMOKERY
7. HEN-DY-EGGS
8. HOOTONS HOMEGROWN
9. PETER HAYWOOD
10. BRETT GARNER
11. MENA JONES
12. LEWIS JONES
13. LLANGYBI ORGANICS
14. MENAI OYSTERS
15. GALLET-Y-BEREN FARM
16. QUIRT FARM
17. SELECTIVE SEAFOODS
18. SOUTH CAERNARFON CREAMERIES LTD
19. HERBS FROM WALES
20. E.T. JONES
21. D & A ELLIS AND SON
22. GLASFRYN PARC FARM SHOP
23. BWDLYN
24. JOYCE AND EMLYN
25. ELWYN
26. MARY GAUNT

The Producers

The producers that I found while travelling this beautiful area, are the real stars to me. Their contribution in these times of globalisation is both inspiring and essential. They offer a lot of hope for the future of local food in the British Isles – they deserve both our respect and support in the future.

Many of them don't farm, fish or produce in large quantities. For example, on the hill in Aberdaron, Joyce and Emlyn have a very small plot of land, yet under not ideal conditions they manage to supply the locals with vegetables and fruit for much of the year. They really care what they produce, growing for flavour not looks. I remember going to pick up a box from her one day and she had placed in six varieties of tomatoes, all delicious and all different in character. I also recall one day when the wind was particularly strong. I'd popped in to say hi, and see if she had any raspberries I could buy. However, it soon became apparent that this wouldn't be possible. The wind had flattened the lot. It was a most depressing sight, and I imagine a lesser soul would have decided not to bother next year. Not Joyce, though, she wouldn't ever consider giving it up, she really gets a buzz out of what she does and offers a direct route to fantastic produce.

Some, however, produce rather more, like South Caenarfon Creamery, which is the largest co-operative in Wales and takes in most of the milk from local farms. There is Shaun at Menai Oysters, who supplies tonnes of mussels and oysters every year from an area that is one of the first registered for farming mussels. Fishermen like Sion Jenkins and Steve Harrison, whose pots catch the delicious lobsters and crabs that have ideal growing conditions in the waters of the Llyn Peninsula. It's great when the sea is calm and the sun is shining, but when it's cold, grey and miserable... not so much fun.

All the people I met on my journey continually inspired me, and they were all more than happy to spend time with me. This naturally made it far easier for me, and gave me a lot of freedom.

I salute you all.

A Guiding Hand

Ethic
Throughout the book it is important to remember that although it is set in North Wales, its ethic is relevant to all of the British Isles. We all have the capacity to shop locally. Initially it will require a little more effort and planning. The more we demand local products in our country, the more they will appear and become easier to find.

One tonne of food in the UK travels an average of 123km before it reaches the shelves... compared with 82km in 1978..

Local
Local food means meeting not only local producers, but local people too. It greatly reduces the distance that your food travels, thus having a positive effect on the environment.

Food which is grown and marketed locally keeps money circulating within the local economy. If your Sunday lunch consists of beef from Australia, runner beans from Thailand, potatoes from Italy, carrots from South Africa, broccoli from Guatemala and fruit from the USA and New Zealand, the ingredients could have travelled 49,000 miles. All of these ingredients are also produced in the UK.

Community
Sourcing your food locally helps you feel part of a community, something real and tangible. It produces a sense of pride in your local area.

No European country is as reliant on supermarkets as is the UK.

Economics
Buying from local producers means that the local area retains

more money to invest in the future.

In 2001, the average farmer earned £5200.

For every one pound spent on an organic box, £2.40 was contributed to the local economy. Only £1.20 was generated from the same amount spent in a supermarket.

Application

This method of shopping should not just be a supplement to your weekly food shop, it should form the backbone of it. The variety and quality of food on offer is increasing all the time. When the apple season is in full swing in our country, the selection available is diverse, and the difference in flavours will remind you that we grow the best apples in the world.

We import over 400,000 tonnes of apples every year, while over 60% of UK apple orchards have been lost since the 1970s.

Supermarkets source only 40% of their apples from the UK at the height of the British season.

There are over 2000 varieties of apples in the national fruit collection at Brogdale in Kent.

Ingredients

The ingredients I have used are what I could source in the local area that I travelled and lived in. You may find that you can use a different fish or cut of meat in a recipe. The beauty of shopping locally is that people will be able to advise on alternatives. I have offered suggestions myself where I saw it was relevant. Always ask questions about the provenance of what you are about to buy – where your meat comes from, what it is fed on, what breed, how old, how long it is hung for...?

If bought at a supermarket, many ingredients may have travelled cumulatively over 24,000 miles. Choosing to buy locally, and thus more likely seasonally, this could be reduced to 376 miles. A whopping 66 times fewer food miles.

Recipes

All the recipes are based on local ingredients, and were cooked in the season in which they were available. Many of them are very simple, and rely on the ingredients being top class. I have occasionally used a few exotic-sounding ingredients, like preserved lemons in a fish tajine (page 14). However, these are items are in the minority.

Remember, you can interpret a recipe as you like – you are in charge of your kitchen, be free to express your own beliefs.

Food transportation comprises 25% of our road traffic. Locally produced and sold food dramatically reduces these food miles.

Adventure

You can treat this book as an adventure, where a new page is turned every day. Hunt out familiar local ingredients and search out the less familiar. You may find that many are under your nose. I found some crab apple trees lining a main road in Brixton, and a damson tree in Peckham, nearby where I live in London.

In 1997 there were no farmers' markets. Now there are over 300.

Seasonal Satisfaction

All food should leave you satisfied, especially if you have sourced and cooked it yourself. The people you cook for should feel warm and happy. Good food is not a once week treat, but an everyday necessity. Cooking seasonally means you buy produce that is at its best, when it is plentiful and when the price is at its most competitive. The sense of excitement that greets the first asparagus, apples or grouse should be felt by everyone. It means there is always something to look forward to.

For every calorie of carrot flown from South Africa, we use 66 calories of fuel.

Real Faces, Real Food

Are you curious where your food comes from? Are you curious about how the beef you are about to eat is raised? Are you curious about the farmers who care for the animals, plant the vegetables and go to sea to hook you a prized bass? If you are, the chances are you have already sought out your nearest farmers' market or farm shop.

Farmers' markets have rapidly increased in popularity over the last five years, great news for farmers everywhere. After so many recent setbacks in farming, notably BSE and foot-and-mouth, these markets offer them the chance to sell their produce directly to us, the consumer. In these days of the supermarkets' global power and sanitised shopping, farmers' markets are an opportunity to release the shackles and get out into the fresh air to explore what's on offer.

The markets can range from the very small – maybe just a few stalls – to the quite large, maybe 40+ stalls. The food offering also varies, but will usually include fresh vegetables, fruit, fish, bread and a few meat stalls. The larger markets are able to go further and offer specialist cheeses, hand-made preserves, cakes, specialist meat suppliers including beef, lamb, pork, mutton, poultry suppliers, game, fresh eggs... even non-food products are offered at some. At Marylebone Farmers' Market, where I trade, there is a fantastic stall selling lavender products... people can't get enough of it!

Good food starts with excellent ingredients, which need to be grown or cared for by people who have passion for what they do. The real people who turn out in all conditions, be it snow, rain, wind or frost, and rarely get any time for themselves. At Christmas when we are all waking up late, feeling the effects of the night before, some of them will have been up for hours tending their animals. Animals need attention all year round, they don't have holidays like the rest of us – they need to be checked and monitored, thus ensuring the farmer is producing the quality he or she requires.

I have had many a funny conversation with farmers about the lack of awareness of the general public towards their role on their farms. Despite this, they are always willing to explain to people exactly what they do, how they go about it and why they continue to do it.

I have spoken to some folk who seem apprehensive to go to food markets. Maybe they are embarrassed because they don't know what to ask for. Perhaps they're wary because things are not wrapped in neat little packages and priced with nice shiny labels. They might even be scared to strike up a conversation with somebody, perish the thought!

Well, my answer to everyone is, don't be shy! Turn up and confront your discomfort, and you'll leave significantly richer for the experience. Farmers' markets are more than just a place to pop out and buy a steak for supper. They offer a chance to get out and mix in the community, shop in pleasant, laid back surroundings and reconnect with the public face of food. Farmers at these markets are very approachable, and are only too willing to have a chat. Many love to explain the qualities of the products they are offering. Go and buy a piece of beef and be told the breed, how it is reared (organic or not), where it was slaughtered, how long it has been hung for, what cut to buy for a particular dish. Go and see the all the great produce on offer, inspect all the varieties of apples (I saw 14 varieties on a stall once, that's about eight more than in the average supermarket). It's a fun experience, educational, and extremely reassuring to shop directly with the people on the cutting edge.

These markets also serve as a reminder of seasonality. These are times of eager anticipation for cooks, awaiting the first asparagus, lush strawberries, spring lamb, grouse and other game birds, delicious sprouting broccoli and juicy sweetcorn picked just the day before.

You will also find many different varieties of certain fruits and vegetables that you can't buy in a supermarket. Strawberries are a classic example. Generally, you may only find Elsanta because they are the right shape, store better and hold for longer without damaging, but that variety lacks any serious flavour. Seek out varieties such as Florence, Flamenco, Kimberly and Hapil, to name a few, and you'll discover a whole new world of strawberries. Flavour is what counts to the growers here, not what shape and size they are. Many of the stallholders will let you sample things before you decide to buy, or simply to enthuse you about what they do.

The farmers and producers at these markets will all generally be from within a thirty mile radius of the market, or in the case of London and larger cities this extends up to a hundred miles to allow for wider diversity. When you buy here you know you are supporting local food, and significantly reducing the miles your food has travelled to reach your plate. You are benefiting from not having your food packaged, which is very costly and damaging to the environment, and this will of course help to reduce waste.

This is what makes farmers' markets special. It makes perfect sense – after all, when you go on holiday to France, Italy or Spain, don't you always enjoy trying the local foods and specialties in the market, and often come back raving about them? Well, it could easily be the same here. The most powerful person in the food world is you – demand more local foods, go and buy them and they will become a regular feature all over the country.

So, the choice is yours – mind-sapping supermarket or the fresh vibrancy of your local farmers' market? If you want to get real food, you need to see the real faces.

Homegrown Heaven

A shocking night's sleep, not helped in the least by the Duke of Edinburgh bunch practicing their impression of the annual wildebeest migration. Wouldn't have minded so much if they had lent a touch more authenticity to proceedings, this is sheep country!

Still, I decide a little chat with them later will do the job, and surely they should be sleeping out in tents anyway? What's going on!

I've spent the night in a youth hostel just outside Bethesda (Idwal Cottage), a cosy little spot and out of season an absolute dream of peace and solitude. It is positioned at the foot of Glyder Fawr, in the Ogwen Valley, an area frequented by many a fell walker and serious rock climbing types. I also indulged in a spot of exercise yesterday, a quick ramble up a mountain – get those lungs working. I normally fell walk with my brothers, and there is a very good reason for this... they know how to read maps and I don't, and I usually eat all their food. Still, I avoid getting lost, manage to have lunch at the top, a little snooze behind some rocks, and get back before it's dark. Simple!

The hostel is run jointly by a young Dutch couple. Now, I happen to really like the Dutch, a very relaxed bunch, they speak great English and know how to ride a bike through a city while extremely drunk. All done with no bash hat and carrying extra passengers... very impressive!

I begin my day with a couple of soft boiled eggs. Three-and-half minutes is how I like mine, toasted soldiers, heavily buttered, cup of tea and a bowl of cornflakes. The eggs are from Hooton's Homegrown on the Isle of Anglesey, my first port of call for today.

I was supposed to go yesterday, but got caught up with a lady talking blue cheese, Margaret Davies from Quirt Farm.

Anglesey used to be known as the 'Bread of Wales', the supplier, the engine room. And although this may not seem to be the case anymore, there is a movement of people here who are dedicated to producing top quality food, and their committment is pushing it to the fore.

Michael and Rosalind Hooton are two such individuals, proprietors of Hooton's Homegrown in Brynsiencyn. Basically, Hooten's is a farm shop, but this term does it no justice. Farm shops are not uncommon, so nothing unusual here you might think. Well, not quite, for about 95% of the items in this shop are produced by themselves. A locally sourced shop, this sounds too good to be true... am I in heaven?

From the outside, however, it looks more like your run of the mill garden centre than a gastronomic outpost; more hanging baskets than home produced guinea fowl. Looks are certainly deceptive in this case. They have been proud owners of this enterprise for the last seven years, although they have been farming for nearly forty and have around 200 acres, 15 of which is set aside for vegetable and fruit growing. This is no mean feat, because these parts are not exactly renowned for growing. They grow 10 varieties of apples, many of which have been neglected by supermarkets (and most of those come from foreign shores).

I'm intrigued by the range Hooten's have on offer – rocket, tomatoes, potatoes, guinea fowl, beef, lamb, cheese, preserves, strawberries, rainbow chard, bacon... and not forgetting Margaret's award winning cheese. Michael more than once stresses the need for variety – shoppers demand it, so they must deliver it, or else the regulars wouldn't bother coming. One of their aims is to supply enough selection so that customers can go away and prepare a complete meal, and a very decent one at that. This is a seasonal haven – if they produce it, they sell it. So where are the autumn raspberries? Rosalind tells me they've failed to yield much this year, disappointing she admits, but that's nature for you.

I'm keen to talk to them about the issue of livestock, and the problems that arise for them. Yet another abattoir has closed, this time on Anglesey, the second one that has closed in a week in these parts. The one in Caenarfon as also recently shut down. Their pigs, lambs and cattle travel 50 miles to the nearest slaughterhouse – too far, says Michael, but what can he do? There is a major lamb abattoir on Anglesey, but it is not suitable for their needs. He says it inevitably adds stress to the animals, costs more in fuel, which not only means more money, but is also is worse for the environment – a point that he cleary feels strongly about.

The chickens he rears can be finished on site, so this isn't a problem, although it is a very time consuming job as it is all done by hand. He keeps them for at least 80 days. They are allowed to roam freely, and are fed a completely natural diet. They sell for between £10 and £12 a bird... hold on a minute, did I hear that right? Can't I buy three or even four chickens for that in the supermarket? You can... but the bird is likely to be flabby, pumped full of water, tasteless when cooked and poor in texture. Still, the choice is yours. Have you ever noticed how much your cheap chicken shrinks in the oven when you cook it? Well, look more closely next time and you will see my point. Roast one of Michael's chickens and the result could not be more different – a full bird, high meat content, hardly any shrinkage, rich flavour, meaty texture, and on completion a totally satisfied feeling. Better to eat one of these than three inferior chickens... just a thought?

So, what about any other family involvement? Well, unusually their three kids are part in the enterprise at the moment – one not exactly by choice – but they hope he might be persuaded to stick with it. The challenge is to keep building something that will be sustainable for the future, that will offer a decent living for the family, and for them to grow into an even stronger position. They are well supported by the local community, one of whom makes the cakes for them. But she is giving it up, so if you are in the area and fancy baking a few cakes, give them a call!

They attend a farmers' market in Colwyn Bay, which is about 50 miles away, an effort they confess doesn't always reap huge rewards, particularly if it is wet and windy. Michael admits that labour is a real issue, and proves a constant challenge. They can have a maximum of 10 employees during the busy period, including students from Europe who come every year. So what about wages? Well, we all know about the minimum wage and why it is there, but apparently the agricultural minimum wage is higher (I also didn't know this). This shocked and surprised me, not that it shouldn't be higher, because the work is very physically demanding, but it does put extra pressure on food producers who are already well up against it.

The Hootens have received no financial help in their enterprise, although they are unstinting in their praise for Mentor Mon, the Anglesey support agency, who have been very encouraging and proactive in supporting local initiatives to a wider audience. They are very proud of their achievement so far, one gained by sheer hard work and determination, and they're looking forward to the future.

My time up, Rosalind hurries back to her jam making duties – there is no end to the talents here. This place really does epitomise the ethic of local sourcing. The future looks fairly bright for them, and I hope they can continue to evolve. We need more places like this. If they can do it in Anglesey, then many more should be able to.

Prince Charles used similar words when he visited them in 2003... great minds, eh?!

fish

An ocean of opportunity... but who's selling?

One of the greatest mysteries to me when I'm around many parts of our coast is not the lack of fish in the ocean, more the lack of places to buy it. Why is this? Surely your average person is not going to track down the local fisherman, make friends, ask them what's available, start asking the price, negotiate, and then wander back to base to prepare their one bass? Most people just simply don't do that, and probably wouldn't know where to start. How many times have you been by the sea and not seen local fish jumping out at you and screaming 'BUY ME', I'm fresh and available? How many fish and chip shops have local catch that they fry, so when you are sitting round the bay or harbour, you can tuck into it, knowing it is adding to your sense of experience and occasion? The best fish and chips I ever had was in New Zealand at the Blue Tuna in Pahia. Two of the freshest John Dory fillets, sealed into the lightest, crispy batter and served with great chips and a generous wedge of lemon.

The fish was first class, suberbly firm flesh, perfectly moist, translucent and tasting like it had just been caught that morning. When I finished, I went up to the two Maori ladies cooking to congratulate them on a sensational supper. Their reply was not one of 'surprise', it wasn't even 'I'm glad you enjoyed it' – they simply wanted to know who was next in the queue! You see, they knew it was good, because it was always good, and it was just another day for them. But for me, it's something to always remember it. John Dory deep fried... now there's a thing?

There have been many times in my early research for this book when I have simply been left scratching my head. There must be more varieties of fish for sale than I had come across? Sure, I could get lobster, crab, oysters and mussels, the occasional bass and mackerel is plentiful at the right time of year, but what of the rest? Where are the other wonders of the culinary sea? Of course, I could easily put a net out in the bay and possibly achieve a decent catch of bass, or trek to the edge of Bardsey Sound, clamber down onto the rocks and cast out a few lines, hoping for some pollack or coley that I'm told is abundant in February. However, it seems that the truth – as Steve Harrison informs me – is that the people in this area are not particulary great fish eaters, and while he himself likes mussels, prawns and black bream, try putting a piece of plaice in front of him and the next day you will see it used as bait for his pots. I can't particularly blame him, though. He uses it for bait all the time – it stinks, and the mere thought of eating this particular fish leaves his stomach churning.

The bottom line is that most of the fish from the waters about here is destined for foreign shores, hoovered up by large vessels from, say, Holland, and then shipped back there for the Dutch to enjoy. Lucky them. I simply can't believe it, other countries fish our waters and we just roll over and let them carry on. Also there is supposed to be a six mile exclusion zone around these waters to stop large vessels fishing. Scallops were being strictly controlled when I arrived back here in early February, so that only certain areas could be fished. Two weeks later this had changed, and a complete ban was put in place, so no scallops could be fished at all. Just a week later a couple of large vessels were spotted dredging well inside the zone, huge dredgers on either side, scraping along the sea bed and destroying everything in their path.

This is supposed to be banned, and so I was glad to hear that they were caught and fined a hefty £30,000 for their efforts. Pure greed, and although the fine seems steep and would hurt a little, I heard that they were straight out again, as if nothing had happened. Scallops used to be plentiful in these waters, and local fisherman have been fishing them for years in a sustainable fashion.

It seems that hardly any white fish is landed from these waters that is destined for the local market. It's all out there... skate, plaice, coley, pollack, brill, bass, grey mullet, mackerel, herrings... the list goes on. In Pwllheli, there are two fishmongers in town, one of which – Pwllheli Seafoods – is located right on the harbour. Fantastic, can't go wrong there surely? Local boats coming in with fish, straight into the shop and then sold on to the public, what could be more simple? If only that were the case. The only local fish on sale the day I visited were bass and mussels, everything else comes from the wholesale market in Manchester. Shaun, who runs the business, told me he would get me a whole skate, but he'd have to ask the fisherman specially to catch one for me. Stone me, I might as well charter a boat for the day, catch a load of fish, buy a huge freezer and stock up. When I run out I can repeat the process, fish guaranteed... but what a hassle!

I paid a visit to Beaumaris on Anglesey one day. This is perhaps one of the most affluent areas on the island, surely they would have a fishmongers here? Well, the butcher sold fish, but it was all frozen and the selection disappointing. What's wrong with people, don't they want fresh fish, or are they simply scared to demand it?

Even in Holyhead, a large fishing port, it seems there is now only one local boat operating these days, and when I find a local fishmongers, it looks so disappointing I can't even be bothered to go in and ask if anything is local... the answers are becoming all too predictable.

They have some tired looking plaice in the window, a few Manx kippers and a few cooked crabs that you couldn't be sure when they were cooked. I love food... get me out of here!

It seems I will have to catch my own after all, and with the help of Steve that is exactly what I did. He had offered to lend me one of his nets to place in the bay here and take my chances.

So one evening he phoned me, and told me he had the net and would pop round so we could go and set it up. Setting nets all depends on the tide and there is a certain area along a beach where they should be placed. We staggered down from the cottage to the bay below, and as soon as we stepped on the sand we could see a net already set up. Steve said he would have liked to have put the net there, a good spot at the end of the beach where bass might hang out. We make our way slightly up the beach, choose a spot and take the net out from the box. We also have two industrial anchors to fix it with. Most people just fix their nets by burying the ends in the sand and weighting it with a huge stone. Professionalism was the order of the day for us, and we would surely be the envy of the beach netting community. Our net is also considerably larger than that further up from us, so this should give us a better chance of catching something. We stretch the net out, untangle a few bits, Steve ties a few things on and then goes in search of a large stone to secure the centre of the net with.

It's just beginning to get dark as we finish, so we leave... and now all we have to do is wait until the morning. Fingers crossed.

The next morning I'm up at 5.30, it's a chilly morning, the car is iced up and the sky clear. Optimistically, I decide to take a bag with me – well you've got to be at this time of the morning.

I take a short cut across the field, down the bank and over the set of rocks before landing on the beach. I see the net immediately, and it looks like my luck is in. I can see at least three fish from here, and it brings a smile to my face. As I get to the net, I can see it is a little better than three. A couple of small dogfish, which are no good to me, but I've got five bass of a decent size. I start to release the bass from the net, which I thought would be really easy. Bass, however, have some sharp fins on them and prove a little more difficult to budge, producing a few cuts on my hands. I also find that the net can easily cut you. My hands are starting to get cold – it's well below freezing and a numbness is taking over.

I can see Steve walking down to the beach now, and he can see that we have done well. He removes the fish from the net with a lot more fluency than me, not really a surprise I suppose.

I send the dogfish back to the sea and make my way back to the cottage, cold but happy, with my catch. Fish at last – now I can finally set about cooking and enjoying the fruits of my labour.

The net is left out for a further three days. I draw a blank the next day, but on day three I have a huge haul of grey mullet and some bass also. It was very windy overnight and the sea has been stirred up, which are conditions that grey mullet thrive in. Nine mullet in total and four bass, top stuff. Steve hopes I know enough recipes for the mullet – he's not a fan, so he takes the bass instead.

The final day I catch a solitary bass and, with the help of my sister who is visiting for the weekend, decide to pack up the net. The tides are changing anyway, so conditions would not be favourable over the next week.

A lot of fish to scale, gut and clean, and I couldn't be happier, although still a little dismayed that I had to resort to catching my own!

So, it seems the fish is out there, and when you simply must have it, you have to resort to any method possible to get your hands on it.

I might set up a stall to sell any excess to the public... now there's a thought!

Poached Bass, Leeks, Carrots & Saffron Cream

Serves 4

4 x 125-150g/5–6oz bass fillet
25g/1oz butter
2 medium carrots (weighing approx 125g), thinly sliced
2 small leeks (weighing about 125g),sliced and washed
2 small shallots, finely sliced
100ml/4fl oz fish stock
100ml/4fl oz dry white wine
Small pinch saffron
150ml/6fl oz double cream
Salt and black pepper

Heat the butter in a pan and add the carrots, leeks and shallots. Cover with a lid and cook very gently, with no colour for about 7–8 minutes. Remove from the heat and leave to one side.

Season the fish with salt and pepper. Pour the stock and wine into a suitable pan to poach the fish. Lay the fish in skin side down. Cover with a lid or buttered paper and poach gently for about 5–7 minutes.

Remove the fish and keep warm.

Add the saffron to the liquor and bring to the boil and reduce by about a third.

Add the double cream and return to the boil. Add the cooked leeks, carrots and shallot and heat through. Check the seasoning and serve with the fish.

Bass & Mussels

Serves 4

This dish held extra significance for me, as it was cooked with bass caught in the net that Steve Harrison had kindly lent me. Quite a successful first haul of seven fish, and among them three small bass. Getting up at 5.30 in the morning, when the temperature is below zero, definitely makes you respect what you are cooking and adds to the fun... even if I couldn't feel my hands when I got back to the cottage!

In this dish the fish is cooked in tomatoes and wine, with extra liquid coming from the mussels. A touch of saffron is added, and the dish has an aniseed touch with the fennel fronds.

2tbsp olive oil
2 small carrots, diced small
4 small shallots, finely sliced
2 cloves garlic, finely sliced
Pinch of saffron
200ml/8fl oz dry white wine
375g/12oz chopped tomatoes
Allow 150g/6oz bass fillet per person
500g/1lb 2oz cleaned mussels
Small sprig of fennel
Salt and black pepper

Heat the olive oil in a wide pan, add the carrots and shallots.

Cover with a lid or plate and cook very gently for 5–7 minutes without colour.

Add the garlic and saffron and cook for a further 2 minutes.

Increase the heat slightly and add the white wine and tomatoes. Bring to the boil and simmer gently for 10 minutes. The sauce should have reduced by about half.

Add the bass fillets, mussels, fennel fronds and season with salt and pepper. A little salt is all you need as the liquid formed by the mussels will add some.

Cover with a lid and cook over a gentle heat for about 10 minutes, or until all the mussels have opened.

Serve with some warm crusty bread to soak up all that juice.

Roast Bass, Rosemary & Sea Salt

Serves 4

Whole roasted fish is a simple delight and a pleasure to eat. The oven is very hot for this dish, and the fierce heat will help the skin to become crispy, yet because the fish is on the bone the flesh will remain very moist. In the summer it is a great thing to cook on the barbeque.

Just before cooking this I decided it would be a good idea to thinly slice some potatoes to sit the fish on, great to eat as they soak up any juices.

1 kg/2lb 8oz bass, cleaned
3 sprigs rosemary
Olive oil
1 dessert spoon sea salt
Black pepper
2 potatoes with skin on, thinly sliced

Put the rosemary in the cavity of the fish and season inside with a little of the salt and pepper.

Place the sliced potatoes on the bottom of the roasting tray, brush with a little olive oil.

Put the fish on top, brush with olive oil and sprinkle with the remaining sea salt.

Place in a hot oven, 220–230ºC/450ºF, gas mark 8 for about 25–30 minutes.

Grey Mullet, Black Olives & Tomatoes

Serves 4

4 x 150g/6oz portions grey mullet fillet
50ml/2fl oz olive oil
1 onion, about 200g/8oz chopped
2 cloves garlic, finely sliced
300g/12oz chopped tomatoes
12 Kalamata olives
Dessert spoon capers
Salt and black pepper

Heat 20ml of the olive oil in a pan, add the onion and cook gently for about 10 minutes until soft.

Add the garlic and cook gently for 2 minutes.

Add the tomatoes, olives, capers and remaining olive oil. Season with salt and pepper. Simmer very gently for 10 minutes.

Heat a non-stick frying pan or heavy cast iron pan. Add a little oil, season the fish and place in the pan skin side down. Cook over a medium to high heat for about 2 minutes. Turn over the fillets and cook for a further 1–2 minutes.

Serve.

Tagine of Fish, Black Olive & Pickled Lemons

Serves 4

1kg/2lb 8oz grey mullet, cut into 8 pieces on the bone
Good splash of olive oil
2 onions, finely sliced
4 cloves garlic, finely sliced
1 tsp ground cumin
$^1/_2$ tsp ground turmeric
$^1/_2$ finger cinnamon stick
$^1/_2$ tsp ground ginger
Good pinch chilli powder
200ml/8fl oz vegetable stock
2 small pickled lemons, chopped
16 Kalamata olives

Heat the pan with the olive oil, add the onions and cook gently with a lid for about 10 minutes.

Add the garlic and all the spices, stir well and cook for a further 3 minutes.

Season the pieces of grey mullet with salt and pepper and add to the pot. Coat with the onions and spices.

Add the vegetable stock, chopped pickled lemons and olives.

Cover with a lid and simmer gently for about 20–25 minutes.

Sewin, Warm Potato Salad

Serves 4

Sewin, otherwise known as sea trout or salmon trout is closely related to the brown trout of rivers and the lake trout of larger inland waters. Like salmon it is a migratory fish, so spends a lot of time in the open sea, where it feeds mainly on crustaceans, which contributes to its pink flesh. It is most often caught in rivers, although mine turned up in my net one day, which was a bit of a bonus and left me with a huge smile on my face. They have been traditionally esteemed in Wales and can grow up to 1 metre/40" in length, although this is exceptional. It is a wonderful fish and deserves to be prepared simply, with little fuss, to allow you to savour its delicate pink flesh.

The potatoes for the salad are boiled, then drained and some of the dressing is immediately added, to allow the potatoes to soak up the oil and lemon. You can do this in advance, keep them warm and add the leaves a few minutes before serving. When I cooked this dish, my sewin, fresh from the water that morning, weighed about 750g. It was perfect for two portions, each fillet weighing about 200g each. I cut mine in half again, but it is not necessary.

4 x 200g/8oz pieces of sewin
750g potatoes, cut into large dice
150ml/6fl oz olive oil
Juice of $^1/_2$ lemon
1 finely chopped shallot
1 tbsp capers
Salt and black pepper
75g/3oz mixed leaves, mizuna, red mustard and rocket

Place the potatoes in a pan, add a little salt and cover with water.

Bring to the boil and simmer gently until just cooked.

Drain well and then place in a large bowl.

Whisk up the olive oil, lemon juice, shallot, capers and seasoning. Add two-thirds of the dressing to the potatoes and cover with foil or cling film.

Brush the skin of the sewin with oil.

Heat a non-stick frying pan and when hot add the sewin skin side down. Cook for about 2 minutes, and then turn over and cook for a further 1 minute. The fish should be nice and pink.

Mix in the leaves to the warm potatoes.

Serve with the fish and remaining dressing.

Poached Sewin with Sorrel Sauce

Serves 4

4 x 150g/6oz pieces of sewin fillet
100ml/4fl oz white wine
100ml/4fl oz fish stock
Salt and pepper
150ml/6fl oz double cream
Juice of $^1/_2$ lemon
50g/2oz sorrel leaves, finely shredded

Season the fish with salt and pepper and gently poach the fish in the white wine and fish stock. You need to make sure the sewin is pink – the cooking time will depend on the thickness of the fish but should take between 3–5 minutes. Remove the fish and keep warm.

Bring the cooking liquor to the boil and reduce by half. Add the double cream and lemon juice, bring back to the boil and reduce so it coats the back of a spoon. Stir in the sorrel and remove from the heat.

Serve.

Steamed Sewin, Fennel Hollandaise

Serves 4

4 x 150g pieces of skinned sewin fillet

Fennel hollandaise
150g/6oz butter
2 egg yolks
2 tbsps water
Lemon juice
Salt and cayenne pepper
1 heaped dessert spoon chopped fennel fronds

Clarify the butter by heating in a small pan until the solids fall to the bottom.

Place the egg yolks, water and a little salt in a heat-proof bowl.

Place over a pan of simmering water and whisk the mixture until it thickens to a light, creamy sabayon. Don't allow it to become too hot, or you risk the proteins in the egg coagulating and producing scrambled egg.

Remove from the heat and whisk in the butter a little at a time. Add some lemon juice, cayenne pepper and the chopped fennel fronds.

Gently steam the pieces of sewin fillet and serve with the hollandaise sauce

Land & Sea Rice

Serves 4

This dish is based very loosely on the principle of the great Spanish dish paella. The ingredients are added in layers, the meat first, followed by the rice, then the grey mullet and mussels and, lastly, the prawns. I usually like to use a good cooking chorizo in this style of cooking, however, to keep it as local as possible, I have substituted by marinating the chicken or pork with some smoked paprika.

Timing is the most critical thing with this dish, so take time and be very organized with your preparation. The amount of liquid you need may vary in this recipe, so add more stock if required.

500g belly pork or 500g (1lb 4oz)legs/thighs of chicken
1 heaped tsp smoked paprika
Olive oil
1 onion, chopped
4 cloves garlic, finely sliced
200ml/8fl oz dry white wine
625ml/1 ^{1}/$_2$ pints light chicken stock
^{1}/$_2$ tsp saffron
200g/8oz chopped tomatoes
1 tbsp tomato paste
1 sprig of rosemary
Good pinch of chilli flakes
Salt and black pepper.
500g/1lb 4oz paella rice
400g/1lb grey mullet fillet, cut into 4 pieces
500g/1lb 4oz mussels, cleaned
100g/4oz raw prawns, shell on

Start by cutting up either the pork into small pieces or chopping the chicken into even size pieces. If I use chicken in this, I like to leave it on the bone.

Marinade the meat in a spoonful of olive oil and the smoked paprika. Place in the fridge for at least 4 hours, but preferably overnight.

Heat a large pan, the wider the better, for this. Heat a generous amount of olive oil and fry the meat until it is lightly browned. Reduce the heat and add the onions and cook gently for about 5 minutes. Add the garlic, white wine, chicken stock, saffron, chopped tomatoes, tomato paste, rosemary and chilli flakes. Bring to the boil and simmer, with a lid, for 30 minutes.

Add the rice to the pan, making sure there is sufficient liquid to cover.

Simmer gently for 20 minutes, stirring occasionally.

Lay the fish on the rice and scatter over the mussels. Cover with a lid and cook gently until the fish is cooked (should be 10 mins approximately)and the mussels are fully opened. Finally, add the prawns, and cook covered for a further 2 minutes.

Turn off the heat and allow the dish to sit for 10 minutes before serving.

Fish Stock

This is the simplest and quickest of stocks to make. Some bones make better stock than others. Sole, turbot and brill bones are excellent and produce a clear, well flavoured liquor. You can use many of the bones from white sea fish, and the odd head will not do any harm either. It is important to cut the vegetables very small to take the maximum flavour in a short time.

1kg/2lb 8oz white fish bones
1 tbsp vegetable oil
1 onion, finely chopped
2 cloves garlic, finely sliced
Small piece of leek, finely diced
50ml/2fl oz dry white wine
1 litre/2 pints water
Few parsley stalks
6 black peppercorns

Heat the oil in a pan and add the onions and leek. Cook very gently with no colour for about 5 minutes..

Add the fish bones and garlic and cook for 2 minutes.

Pour in the wine, water, parsley stalks and black peppercorns.

Bring to the boil, remove any scum that rises to the surface and then simmer gently for about 20 minutes.

Strain through a fine sieve and use as required.

Pots of Fulfilment

When I first see Sion Jenkins I'm parking the car at Porth Colmon. He's a solitary figure in his tractor, reversing his small fishing vessel into the sea – his office. He appears an unassuming sort of chap, quiet type, I guess, indeed nothing remarkable at all feature-wise. He's dressed in thick, yellow, highly waterproof overalls and sturdy looking wellie boots. Me, well, nothing so grand for me... an old pair of borrowed wellies that seem five times too big, average standard fell walking waterproofs, shades, and my battered but proud green Tillie hat. Weather permitting, this is a daily routine for Sion, although these days he's among a dying breed, not only fighting nature's elements but the human element too.

It's an absolute cracker of a day, picture postcard indeed – sun beaming down on the still, shimmering, bluey-green ocean. Is this really North Wales?

Now, you may be thinking that Sion is an old, wise sea dog, who has a beard, smokes a pipe and recites stories form the good old days. Well, wise he is, old he is not, only 30 years on the clock – but the sea is in his blood, and he has a genuine passion for it, as I was about to find out.

Time for the off. Sion ushers me aboard, at which point I discover I've got a bloody great big hole in my boots... hmm, my old scout master would not have been impressed. Oh well, never mind, no use complaining.

Sion briefly explains what he will be doing today, approximately how long we will be out, how far we are going and expected conditions. He has been doing this for about 18 years, the last four being full time, and he never considers giving it up – he'd have no other clue what to do anyway. This is life for Sion, and as we cruise out of the bay, you can see him slowly changing, like an inner peace has joined him, totally relaxed in the surroundings. Who can blame him? The backdrop is incredible, miles of unspoilt dramatic coastline, views of the mountain ranges of Snowdonia, and further round the famous land that is Bardsey Island, haven for wildlife, including many birds, seals, porpoises and dolphins. He also tells me, somewhat proudly, that the island was the scene of an illegal rave recently... must have made a packet out of return journeys... wonder how Fatboy Slim got over there, just a vicious rumour!

Sion's main business at sea is catching lobsters and crabs, although he also occasionally fishes for bass, grey mullet, herrings and mackerel. This is a seasonal profession, one more or less dictated by nature but increasingly manipulated by other powers. September is not the best time for him. He's quite philosophical about it, though, and says he's had a pretty good year. We reach the site of his first pots, all carefully marked out with little buoys, and he fixes the first rope to the winch, explaining that a few years ago he would have done this all by hand, that means dragging pots from sometimes depths of 70 metres. No need for him to have gym membership then! It's incredibly hard work, and Sion is grateful for the winch which lessens the burden. In all, he has about 200 pots, although some are much further out and we won't be venturing that far today. Not a great haul from the first dozen pots, although there is a common theme to them all, *dogfish*, bloody loads of them. These are a member of the shark family, and are commonly known as huss. Sion has no use for them and flings them back in. These creatures fetch just 15 pence a kilo at Holyhead market on Anglesey, reason enough for him to abandon them to the ocean. I, however ask him to keep me a few of the larger ones. I've cooked with it a little before, and ok, it wouldn't be on top of the list, but as a former head chef of mine said, there's the challenge! He told me that a good cook can master a fillet of bass, but a great cook can conjure something from anything – in this case the dustbin of the ocean, dogfish.

Sion's money is made in lobster, at the moment the price is quite low, around £9.00 per kilo, however at Christmas this rises sharply to as high as £22.00 a kilo. Crabs fetch far less of a premium, around £1.50 a kilo at the moment. Good job I prefer crab, then, isn't it! Sion says he might be lucky to get 10 lobsters today – I do a quick estimate, working out that it means he will receive approx £60. He's also only allowed to take creatures of a certain size, and he frequently measures ones that he considers borderline. Sion says this is really only common sense, and benefits everyone in the future. Something else that benefits everyone is the conservation effort that is in place here. He explains this as he is showing me a female lobster (also known as a hen). This one is carrying eggs, and Sion shows me a mark on her tail. It's been clipped by conservation workers in a drive to sustain stocks.

When the fishermen catch one they tag their claw and put them back. Then they record this and inform the relevant people. He gets paid for that lobster, but in future, he can catch it again and sell it. Obviously he doesn't mind this as he gets paid twice. He also knows that this will hopefully maintain a healthy stock for him in the future, thus protecting his interests. This strikes me as a great scheme, its only drawback is that I can't see the big boys bowing to that one. Sion knows they don't, so nods in agreement. He says the problem has never really been the local fishermen from the small communities around here, most of them merely did it for a little extra income. The problem is the bigger vessels that are allowed closer than they should be. A few years ago they were fighting for a six mile exclusion zone for bigger vessels, to protect the fragile environment around their shores and to help maintain a healthy fish population.

The battle was with the EU, who were seemingly uninterested in hearing any protests put forward, even though the local fishing authority got involved and strongly advised them against this course of action. Guess what? The EU won, what a surprise. Sion tells me they have no interest in the smaller people who have been fishing these waters for generations, it is simply too much hassle for them to govern. Now, here is the crazy thing. A few years ago, the EU raised the maximum number of baskets that anyone could keep to 200. I bet they thought they were being smart, but do you know what people did? They swiftly went out and bought more pots to make their number up to 200. Boom time for basket makers everywhere. In fact, one guy is so busy he had to take on another eight staff to help him keep up with demand! EU = Ecologically Unsound.

On a good day, Sion might expect to collect up to 80 lobsters and five large baskets of crabs. Today he will be lucky to get 15 of the dark blue gems, and two baskets of their poorer cousins. He turns the boat around and starts to head back, time's getting on and although it looks really calm, the waters round these parts are notorious for changing and have caught many a person out... mostly tourists, I'm told. I'm still busy marvelling at how crystal clear the water here is when Sion calmly informs me that we have some visitors. He points to a spot in the water and I'm nodding, making out like I can see what he can see, but I can't. He's spotted three pairs of dolphins, and I am immediately excited, all thought of lobsters and crabs having swiftly gone out the window. Surely I can't be this lucky? But then I spot them, brilliant! What a bonus. Apparently there are regular sightings of them here. Sion carries on what he is doing, while I am completely transfixed.

On the way back he also shows me the site of an old wreck that went down here in 1901. It was carrying a large consignment of whiskey from New Zealand, which was so potent that when the locals recovered it, many died from alcohol poisoning!

The previous night he had placed a net in one of the bays to catch bass. Well, no danger of the net giving way under this haul of fish. In total we got one mackerel and one herring. Can't win them all.

The final task of the day is to find out how many crabs and lobsters one of his customers wants. He sells them mainly to Selective Seafoods, owned and run by Mary and Gareth White in Tudweiliog. He has a good relationship with them, and they pay him a fair price. Cutting out the middle man is a survival technique that becomes a common theme throughout my travels.

Out comes the mobile phone... bloody get everywhere, is nothing sacred!

We've been at sea just over four hours, so is he disappointed with today's catch? Of course he would love more, but here is a man who knows that when the seasons and nature are in his favour, he will be back later to scoop many a grand lobster from his pots.

Sion packs me off with some dogfish, some unwanted spider crabs (no market for these either, criminal) and some normal crabs. These I unleash in the boot of my hire car and, as I leave, I'm thinking of a fish stew with all my goodies.

I'm thrilled with my day and thrilled to have met such a dedicated character, for this is a simple life that gives him enormous pleasure and he never gets bored. For him every day is different, for every day the ocean tells a different story and weaves a bit more magic. You have to love that, don't you?

Crab on Toast

I love freshly boiled crab, cracking the claws to reveal all that sweet, tasty meat. I usually eat about half of it before it even gets near to a recipe. Never throw the shells away, they make an excellent soup or stock.

Crack 2 medium crab claws and pick out the meat.

Check that you have no bones in it and then mix it with a little mayonnaise to bind. Sprinkle in some cracked black pepper.

Toast some slices of good thick white or brown bread. Spread with a little butter and spread over some crab mix. Have some small pieces of lemon ready to squeeze over.

Crab Cakes with Lemon & Caper Mayonnaise

Serves 4

Crab cakes
1kg/2lb potatoes, cooked and mashed
300g/12oz white crab meat
100g/4oz brown crab meat
1 shallot, finely chopped
1 tbsp chopped flat leaf parsley
1 tsp bronze fennel fronds
Salt and black pepper

Mix all the ingredients together and then divide into 8 balls. Shape them into cakes and pass them through some flour. Dust off any excess and then coat them in a light egg wash. Finally, through breadcrumbs. Heat some vegetable oil in a frying pan and shallow fry the cakes for about 3 minutes on each side. Drain on kitchen paper. Transfer to a tray and cook in an oven for 5–7 minutes, 200°C/400°F, gas mark 6.

Lemon & caper mayonnaise
1 egg yolk
$^1/_2$ tsp Dijon mustard
1 dessert spoon white wine vinegar
3 dessert spoons lemon juice
125 ml/5fl oz sunflower/vegetable oil
100ml/4fl oz olive oil
1 heaped dessert spoon of capers
Salt and pepper

Put the egg yolk in a bowl with the mustard, white wine vinegar, salt and lemon juice. Mix together with a whisk. Slowly whisk in the sunflower oil a little at a time, then add the olive oil. Stir in the capers and season with pepper.

Crab Stock

1.4kg/3lb crab shells
Good splash of olive oil
1 medium onion, chopped
2 medium carrots, chopped
6 cloves garlic, sliced
1 tsp dried tarragon
2 star anise
1 strip of lemon peel
1 strip orange peel
Pinch saffron
150ml/6fl oz dry white wine
200g/8oz chopped tomatoes
1 tbsp tomato purée
1 $^1/_2$ litres/3 pints light chicken or vegetable stock
6 black peppercorns

Place the shells in an old tea towel and wrap up. Using a rolling pin, smash up the shells for a few minutes.

Heat the olive oil in a large pan and add the crab shells and fry for about 5 minutes over a medium heat.

Add the onion, carrots and garlic, cover with a lid and cook over a low heat for about 10 minutes. You may need to stir occasionally.

Add the remaining ingredients, bring to the boil and then simmer very gently for about 40 minutes. Do not allow to boil rapidly, as this will produce a bitter result to the stock. Remove from the heat.

Pass through a coarse sieve and then if you like no bits at all, through a fine sieve. Use as required.

Crab Broth

This is a great way to use up the shells from the crab and make it all a bit more economical. You can use prawn and lobster shells in the same way. Smashing up crab shells with a rolling pin is amazingly therapeutic as well!

A great reserve to keep in small batches in the freezer for dishes such as the lobster and bass pot and the tagliatelle with crab and broad beans. You can also have this as a soup – just add some cream and maybe a touch of brandy at the end.

2 tbsps olive oil
Shells of 2 medium crabs
3 cloves garlic, peeled and cut into thin slices
4 small shallots, peeled and finely sliced
1 carrot, peeled and diced
1 tbsp plain flour
1 tbsp tomato purée
200ml/8fl oz dry white wine
1 litre/2 pints water
4 black peppercorns
Few small sprigs rosemary, thyme and parsley
6 fennel seeds
Sea salt

Place the crab shells in an old tea towel. Wrap tightly and using a rolling pin, smash them about a little until they are broken up. This should take you about 2–3 minutes, depending on your mood!

Heat a large pan add the olive oil, when it is quite hot, put the crab shells in and coat with the oil. Fry over a high meat for about 3–4 minutes.

Add the garlic, shallots and carrot, stir these in and reduce the heat and allow to cook gently for about 5 minutes.

Mix in the flour and tomato purée and cook for a further 3 minutes.

Add the wine, increase the heat and stir in well.

Add the remaining ingredients and bring slowly to the boil.

Reduce the heat and simmer very, very gently for about 30 minutes. Do not allow to boil rapidly or it may become bitter.

Pass through a coarse sieve.

Use as required.

Tagliatelle with Crab & Broad Beans

Serves 4

Making fresh pasta is both simple and really satisfying. Good flour is essential, I've used Italian 00 flour, which is sympathecially milled from Durum Wheat. I would love to have used flour milled in our country, so it is regretful we don't produce a similar flour.

400g/1lb 00 soft wheat flour
4 medium eggs, whisked

Tip the flour onto a clean work surface and make a large well. Pour in the eggs and gradually incorporate into the flour. You need to knead this for about 10-15 minutes, until it is smooth and quite tight. Using a pasta machine roll the dough through the 1st setting, do this twice. Then repeat once through the 3, 5 and 6 settings. If you like it a little thicker finish on setting 5. Now pass the rolled dough through the tagliatelle attachment.

A quantity of fresh pasta recipe, rolled into tagliatelle
White crab from a medium crab
125g/5oz shelled, blanched broad beans
Small handful of torn basil leaves
200ml/8fl oz crab stock
50ml/2fl oz olive oil

Heat the crab stock with the olive oil and boil rapidly until the two are emulsified.

Boil the pasta in boiling salted water for 2–3 minutes until al dente. Drain and add to the sauce.

Add the crab, beans and basil leaves. Mix gently together and serve.

Grilled Rockling, Lemon & Parsley Crumb

Serves 4

There are several members of the rockling family, which are related to the cod family. It is a reddish fish with distinctive brown blotches. They have three tiny barbells which they use to grope around for food. They only have a maximum size of about 50cm and a relatively long body.

I came across them one day when I was out with Steve Harrison. A few kept appearing in the lobster pots, so I asked if I could keep them to cook with. He seemed to think they had quite a good flavour, although he doesn't know many people who eat them.

I decided to fillet all of them, they have lots of little bones running through the centre, so were quite fiddly. The white flesh is quite delicate and tastes pretty good.

This is a simple recipe, where the fish is dipped in olive oil and then a mixture of parsley, lemon zest and breadcrumbs are pushed onto the fillets.

I doubt you will ever see these for sale, as there isn't a commercial market for them. You could use whiting, red mullet or even bass for this recipe.

8 fillets rockling, skinned
25g/1oz white breadcrumbs
Zest of $^1/_2$ lemon
2 tbsps chopped parsley
2 tbsps olive oil
1 crushed clove of garlic
Salt and pepper

Mix the breadcrumbs with the lemon zest, parsley, olive oil, garlic and seasoning.

Lightly dip the fish fillets in olive oil and then lightly press some of the crumb mix onto them.

Place them on a tray and then cook them under a hot grill for about 5 minutes, when the fillets should be nice and brown.

Roast Lobster, Herb Butter

Serves 2

For this you need to split the lobsters in half while they are still alive. If you are efficient with your knife the lobsters will die immediately, so don't worry. If you really can't stand the idea of this, you can boil them for about 9–10 minutes and then cut them in half and finish them in a very hot oven or under the grill.

2 lobsters, weighing about 750g/1lb 14oz each
Melted butter for basting the lobster
100g/4 oz softened butter
25g/1oz chopped soft herbs (chives, tarragon and parsley)
Salt and black pepper
Juice of 1 lemon

To split the lobsters in half, place it on a chopping board and using a large, heavy, sharp knife drive the knife through the centre of the cross located on the top of the head. Cut down to the tail and finish at the head, dividing the lobster. Remove the claws and take off the rubber bands. Crack open all three parts of the claw with the heaviest part of the knife.

Place the lobster in a roasting tray, brush with plenty of melted butter and season with salt and pepper.

Mix up the softened butter with the herbs and lemon juice.

Place in a hot oven at 220ºC/425ºF, gas mark 7 and cook for about 8–10 minutes. Add the butter to the lobster for the last 2 minutes and baste to cover

Lobster & Bass Pot

Serves 2–4

Lobster and bass are plentiful in the waters of the Llyn Peninsula. The locals really care about the coastline and the lobsters are first class.

Bass is much sought after by chefs and keen cooks everywhere. However, bass stocks are under pressure in some areas, so try to explore other fish sometimes that don't get as much coverage.

I went to Mary White at Selective Seafoods in Tudweiliog for the lobster and bass. This is where most of Sion's catch ends up. Others sell them, just look out for the signs along the road – this could be an arrow with a fish or a chalkboard.

Most lobsters in this country come from Canada, where it is a massive industry. The price is almost always cheaper, except at times of the year when native lobsters are more plentiful. I find the quality far inferior and the flavour just doesn't deliver.

The lobster in this recipe is cut in half and needs to serve four, so be courteous to your fellow diners.

The bass is left on the bone, which will add more flavour to the pot, and help retain the moisture of the fish.

The pot is thickened by driving together the oil and liquid at a high heat. This is similar to how the classic stew bouillabaisse from southern France is thickened.

1 medium live lobster, split in half
1 x 650–700g/1lb 10oz–1lb 12oz bass, scaled, gutted and cut
* into 4 pieces.*

---

1 red onion, peeled and diced
3 small Cara potatoes, sliced
2 medium tomatoes, chopped
500ml/20 fl oz/1 pint crab broth (see page 31)
50ml/2fl oz olive oil
1 strip orange peel
1 strip lemon peel
Salt
Black pepper
Good handful of basil leaves

Choose a suitable wide and fairly deep pan with a lid.

Heat a tablespoon of the olive oil and gently sauté the onion and potatoes for 5 minutes over a medium heat.

Add the tomatoes, crab broth, remaining oil, orange and lemon peel.

Boil rapidly for 5 minutes to allow the oil to emulsify with the liquid.

Reduce the heat and add the pieces of bass, cover with a lid and cook gently for about 10 minutes.

Add the lobster, cover with the lid again and continue cooking for 5–7 minutes.

Stir in the basil leaves.

Llyn Mon Fish Stew

Serves 4

The grey mullet from my net in Aberdaron Bay, the crab from the waters of the Llyn Peninsula and the mussels from the Menai Straits make up this fish stew, which has some crisp croutons put on at the end – great when soaked with all the fish juices.

1kg/2lb 8oz grey mullet, cleaned and cut into pieces on the bone
500g/1lb 4oz mussels, cleaned
100g/4oz white crab meat
25 ml/1fl oz olive oil
1 onion, chopped
4 cloves garlic, finely sliced
350ml/14 fl oz crab stock
1 tbsp picked fennel fronds
Salt and black pepper
2 thick slices of bread

Cut each slice of bread into 4 pieces and place in a tray. Sprinkle with a little olive oil and some sea salt. Place in the oven at about 200°C/gas mark 6 for about 10 minutes or until golden brown and crispy. Cook the onions gently in the olive oil for about 10 minutes or until soft. Add the garlic and cook for a few minutes. Add the crab stock, bring to the boil and reduce by about a third. Add the grey mullet pieces and some seasoning. Reduce the heat and cover with a lid and cook very gently for 10 minutes.

Add the mussels and cover with the lid and cook gently until they are all open. Add the crab meat, fennel fronds and stir into the stew. Cook for a few minutes to heat through the crab.

Top with the croutons and serve.

Fish Pie

Serves 4

It was a bit of a flick up between using the small rockling I had or grey mullet for this recipe. I decided to use the rockling, which I cut into as big a pieces as I could. I used a few of the local prawns and some white crab meat to improve the depth of flavour. You can substitute the rockling for whiting, pollack, coley, monkfish or cod.

Instead of mash potato, I boiled some Romano potatoes in their skins, peeled them and then sliced them for the top.

500g/1lb 4oz potatoes, washed
750g/1lb 14oz rockling fillet, cut into large pieces
50g/2oz white crab meat
100g/4oz peeled prawns
50g/2 oz chopped shallot or onion
25g/1oz butter
25g/1oz plain flour
100ml/4fl oz dry white wine
200ml/ 8fl oz fish stock, hot
200ml/8fl oz double cream
1 tbsp mixed chopped fennel and parsley
Salt and black pepper

Boil the potatoes gently until they are almost cooked, remove and allow to cool.

Melt the butter in a pan and add the shallot or onion and cook gently until soft. Add the flour and mix in well to make a roux. Cook over a gentle heat for 2–3 minutes.

Increase the heat slightly and add the wine and mix until smooth, then gradually add the hot stock, stirring all the time until smooth.

Add the double cream and some seasoning. Bring to the boil and simmer gently for 5 minutes.

Peel and slice the potatoes.

Put the fish, crab meat and prawns into a pie dish and sprinkle with the herbs.

Pour over the sauce and then layer over the potatoes.

Bake in the oven at 200ºC/400ºF, gas mark 6 for 35 minutes.

Menai Oysters

Phew, just made it, running late again. Usually if someone tells me the nearest pub, I'm fine, and then if you get lost, you can easily console yourself with a pint.

On my arrival Shaun is already manoeuvring his shiny new tractor out of its resting place, near the large shed where he sorts his oysters and mussels. No time for any casual chit chat, just a quick introduction and then I'm back in my car following him down the lane and out onto the main road. We are heading down to the straits, where he farms his oysters and mussels. A bit of maintenance work and some collecting to do today. Timing is critical, as he must catch the tides right and allow himself enough time to complete his given tasks. I'm hoping to give him a hand, and have come equipped with my brand new green, hardcore wellies... no more wet feet for me!

On arrival, Shaun instructed me to park in a certain place, so I decided to ignore this and find my own space, more fool me. I look to see where he has positioned his tractor on the grey muddy beach and discover that he is miles away. I start the long trudge over, but it's slow going, lifting my feet out of the sludge. Shaun is laughing when I reach him, the kind of smug, wise laughter we all love to hate.

He started this business, along with his father, nearly 10 years ago, and he leases a considerable area of land and water on the Menai Straits. Originally, he just farmed oysters, but by their nature they are not the fastest growing species. So five years ago he started to farm mussels. He found there were a lot of mussels already when he started, and told me they used to be farmed here but for years had been neglected. It took him a long time and a lot of hard work to clean it all up. Now mussels are the main part of his business, and at the moment he shifts about 3.6 tonnes a week, most of which end up in the north-west. He has an excellent relationship with M&J Seafoods, who are now a very big company. He has known them for years, though when they were a lot smaller and they treated him well. Not that he would stand for it any other way, he doesn't appear the sort to get messed around, and will openly speak his mind if he has a problem with a supplier.

He loves it out here, which for an outsider is quite hard to understand, particularly on such a grey, miserable day as this. He loves the peace and isolation it offers him, thriving on his work, a highly motivated individual. He's an enthusiastic supporter of the food movement on Anglesey, which is beginning to really take shape, and he's optimistic for the future.

One of his plans is to open a café nearby, overlooking his harvesting area. What better way to celebrate local success, than to sell your mussels and oysters from the source? It makes total sense. During the tourist season, Anglesey receives many visitors, and this would allow him to show off his quality product. Apparently there used to be a café/fishmonger just near the Menai Bridge, that cooked and sold local fish and seafood. This closed down a while ago, and now there is nothing. This, unfortunately, is not uncommon in our country. Have people forgotten what they have on their doorstep? Shaun puts a lot of it down to ignorance and lack of support for local foods, although this is slowly changing.

He is proud of his achievements so far. He's built a business slowly, one that will be sustainable in the future. He spends at least 3–4 days a week down here, tending the beds, and the work is extremely physically demanding. He lifts tremendous weights every day, and confesses he has no need for gym membership.

It sometimes surprises me that great food comes from such mucky looking waters. This, as Shaun points out, is ideal for growing oysters, they thrive in these conditions.

Back at base, he shows me some of the new equipment he has

invested in. There's a new oyster grader, a new filter system for both the oysters and mussels. He also shows me some of the old equipment he and his dad used in the early days, basic, cheap but very effective. They look rickety and totally worn out now, but stand as a gentle reminder of the foundations and how far they have come.

Time to head back to my hostel, the drive will give me an opportunity to think of the many things I will cook with the bag of mussels, and time enough to realise that I don't have a knife to shuck my oysters with! Still, a good cook should never blame his tools.

Mussels, Beer & Chips

Serves 4

The beer for this comes from Anglesey, and is I believe a fine drinking example. I must admit to not ever quite finding the taste for real ale, something I'm actually quite sad about. I used it with good results in this dish of mussels and beer though. Real comfort food, quick to make, great to share and washed down with the rest of the beer.

On this particular day I used Romano potatoes to make the chips and fried them in a mixture of beef dripping and vegetable oil. Finally, I sprinkled them with a little vinegar and some Anglesey sea salt.

Note on Mussels

To prepare your mussels, place them in the sink or a large bowl. Wash them in plenty of cold water and repeat if they are really dirty. Scrape the mussels with a short thick blade knife, removing any barnacles and then pull out the beard. Always discard any that are damaged. Cooking mussels is very simple, quick cooking over a high heat is all that is required. Any that do not fully opened should be discarded.

1kg/2lb 8oz mussels, cleaned
1 onion, finely chopped
1 small leek, finely sliced
2 cloves garlic, finely sliced
150ml/6fl oz beer
150ml/6fl oz double cream
Black pepper

Sweat the leeks in a large pan with a little vegetable oil.

Add the mussels and increase the heat. Add the garlic, beer and a few good twists of black pepper. Cover with a lid and cook over a high heat until all the mussels are opened.

Tip the mussels into a colander and reserve the liquor.

Put the liquor back in the pan and reduce by about half. Add the double cream and bring to the boil. Put the mussels back in the pan, heat through and serve.

For the chips

If you have a small pan, fry the chips in batches, so not to overcrowd and make your potatoes go mushy.

1kg/2lb 8oz potatoes, cut into even size chips
Beef dripping and vegetable oil to fry

Heat the fat to about 140ºC and blanch the potatoes in the oil until they are soft. Remove and drain the potatoes.

Increase the heat to 180ºC and fry the chips until they are golden brown and crispy.

Drain on kitchen paper.

Serve sprinkled with sea salt and vinegar.

Mussels & Leeks

Serves 4

1 kg/2lb 8oz mussels, cleaned
Splash of olive oil
2 shallots, finely sliced
1 small leek, split in half lengthways and finely sliced
50ml/2fl oz white wine
1 clove garlic
Black pepper
50ml/2 fl oz double cream

Heat a suitable pan and add the olive oil, shallots and leek. Cover with a lid and cook very gently for about 5 minutes or until the leeks have softened slightly.

Add the garlic, mussels, white wine and pepper. Increase the heat and cover with a lid.

Steam the mussels until they have opened and then add the cream. Bring to the boil, shake the mussels about in the liquid and serve.

Menai Mussel & Potato Soup

Serves 4-6

1kg/2lb 8oz mussels, cleaned
25g/1oz butter
150g/6oz chopped onion
60g/2 /₂ oz diced bacon
3 cloves garlic, finely sliced
200g/8oz peeled and diced potato, not washed
400ml/16 fl oz milk
Liquor from the mussels (about 200ml/8 fl oz)
Small piece of bay leaf
Salt and black pepper
100ml/4fl oz double cream
A little chopped parsley

Steam the mussels open in a little white wine. Drain and reserve the cooking liquor. Let the mussels cool slightly, then remove the meat from the shells.

In a saucepan sweat the onions and bacon in the butter for about 10 minutes.

Add the garlic and potatoes and cook for about 3 minutes.

Add the mussel cooking liquor, milk, bay leaf, a little salt and black pepper. Bring to the boil and simmer very gently for about 25 minutes or until the potatoes are cooked.

Add the double cream, mussels and some chopped parsley. Stir and serve.

Mussel, Leek & Saffron Tart

Serves 8

1kg/2lb 8oz mussels, steamed and shelled
Knob of butter
2 small leeks, washed and finely sliced
1/₂ red onion, finely sliced
Good pinch of saffron
100ml/4fl oz milk
200ml /8fl oz double cream
3 eggs
Salt and black pepper

1 recipe short crust pastry (see p. 147)

Line a loose bottom 8"/20cm tart tin with the pastry. Bake blind in the oven at 200ºC/400ºF gas mark 6 for 10 minutes.

Heat a saucepan, add the butter, the leeks and the onion. Stir well and add the saffron. Cover with a lid and cook gently for about 10 minutes or until the leeks and onions have softened slightly. Remove from the heat.

In a bowl whisk up the eggs, milk, cream and seasoning. Place the leeks in the tart case, add the mussels and pour over the egg mix.

Place in the oven at 200ºC/400ºF gas mark 6 for about 25 minutes or until lightly brown and set.

Spaghetti & Mussels

Serves 4

1kg/2lb 8oz mussels, cleaned
50ml/2fl oz dry white wine
Splash of olive oil
2 cloves garlic, crushed
200g/8oz chopped tomatoes
1 tsp tomato paste
Pinch crushed chilli flakes
Salt and black pepper
200g/8oz spaghetti
4 tbsps green sauce (optional – see p. 72)

Place the mussels and the white wine in pan, cover with a lid and cook over a high heat until all the mussels are opened. Drain them in a colander and reserve the liquor. Allow the mussels to cool slightly and then remove from their shells.

Cook the spaghetti in plenty of boiling salted water.

While the pasta is cooking, heat the olive oil in a pan and gently cook the garlic for 2 minutes. Add the cooking liquor from the mussels, chopped tomatoes, tomato paste, chilli flakes. Bring to the boil and then simmer gently for about 10–15 minutes. The sauce should be reduced by about half. Add salt and pepper if required.
Add the mussels and heat through for 2–3 minutes.

Drain the pasta.

Add the pasta to the sauce and mix together.

Serve with the green sauce.

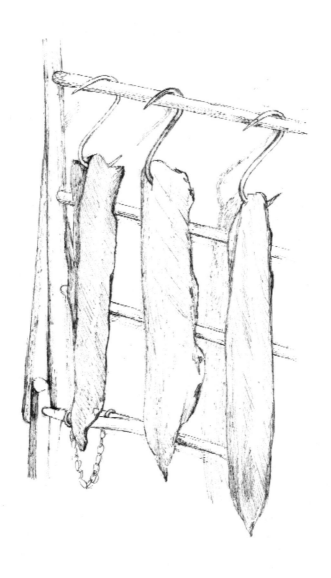

A dustbin, wood chippings and a fish?

As you drive into the cottage I stayed at in Aberdaron, right in front of you is a garage, not huge but sufficient to get a normal sized motor in. The outside of it is a bit shabby, with a few gaping holes to the left side, and once you've pulled back the panelled wood doors, you step inside to a similar story. This is the place to store the coal, logs, fishing gear, any odds-and-sods that are not welcome... and a couple of old dustbins. One was in pretty good condition, whilst the other one was a bit of a wreck, and if keeping up appearances is your bag, not one to display in front of your neighbours. To me, however, it would prove to be very useful indeed, especially when I had an excess of fish and maybe a few other bits and pieces.

I decided to construct my own smoking vessel to preserve any fish that might potentially end up in a decent bin. Actually, the catalyst for my actions was more down to a stray comment I threw Steve Harrison on one of my fishing trips with him.

One weekend I had driven back to London to have a little time away from the research and writing. On my return it was a very cold, clear, frosty night in February, and I arrived very late, at around midnight. After opening the gates to the cottage, I drove the few feet to position the car. As I jumped back in the car I could have sworn I saw something hanging on or near the back door of the house, so I got out to investigate. And there it was, a bloody great big conger eel, a large hook through its neck and a little bit frozen to say the least. A few weird thoughts immediately went through my head – could it be a some strange ritual that they practice on strangers from out of town, or was it simply a spiritual giving, a kind of sympathetic gesture for beating us in the rugby? I racked my brain, but that night I drew a blank. I unhooked the fish, chopped it in half and stored it in the fridge.

In the morning I remembered that I'd vaguely asked Steve to get me a conger eel if he happened upon one. He denied any knowledge of it at first, but after letting me sweat a bit he finally owned up.

Smoking food is one of our oldest ways of preserving food, and there are people who have far more knowledge and expertise than me. David at Deri-Mon Smokery produces fish, meats and cheeses of the highest quality. So why bother? Well, there's something very satisfying about producing something from start to finish, catching your own fish, preparing and finally cooking them – or more specifically, smoking them.

In addition to the eel, I had some grey mullet, sewin, bass and even some dogfish to play around with, so I decided to hot smoke and cold smoke some of each. The process of smoking fish is relatively straightforward, although a few strict rules must be adhered to. Your fish must be in first class condition, and because smoking does not fully cure the fish, you must cure it first – which in its most simple form means spreading it with a combination of sea salt and sugar. You must also rinse the fish, dry it well and then hang it in a dry, cool place for about 24 hours. Make sure you use the right wood chippings – hard woods such as oak, cherry, apple and pear are good, and some such as pine are to be avoided, as they'll leave your fish tasting harsh and bitter. Finally, you must decide what end product you need, hot or cold smoked. This will determine the temperature your smoker must be at, and how long they must stay in for. Cold smoking requires a temperature of around 28ºC/82ºF, and it will not alter the texture of the end product, as the flesh remains raw. Hot smoking requires a temperature of 55ºC/130ºF, and it will leave the flesh semi or fully cooked. It generally needs less time in the smoker than something that is cold smoked.

Unfortunately, I didn't have the luxury of a temperature gauge, so I had to employ 'trial and error'!

To prepare my dustbin I removed the base, which was almost off anyway, and made some small holes in it. I then wedged this back into the bin and pushed it into place, about 12–14cm from the bottom. Then I found an old disposable barbeque tray, which would prove perfect to make my fire in. I threw in a little coal, a crumbled fire lighter and bingo, one small fire.

Once the fire is lit and the coals are nice and hot, it is time for the wood chippings, oak in my case. These go on the coals and you place the tray under the bin, then you're ready to go. The old base with the holes in it acts as a natural barrier to the smoke, and allows it to filter through slowly and more evenly.

Now, this is the most critical point, the temperature. I covered the bin tightly with tin foil and left it for half and hour. For cold smoking I would test it by touching the outside of the bin, which if it was about right should feel lukewarm. I then removed the foil and made sure the smoke was not too fierce. If too hot, I'd simply take some oak dust and smother the fire at the bottom, hopefully cooling it sufficiently to carry on with the smoking.

Then I had to find something to hang my fish from in the top of the smoker. For this I used an old cooling wire that I found in a charity shop in Caenarfon. I collected my fish from just inside the back door, where it was on hooks hanging from a clothes horse. My first effort was the grey mullet, sewin and bass, which I smoked for about three hours. It came out surprisingly well, although I'll confess to being paranoid about it being too hot, and was constantly leaving the comfort of the cottage to check on its progress. From then on I smoked lots more food, and experimented with different cures and flavours in the fire. The whole process leaves you feeling really good, and I'll admit it to being really proud of myself.

Now, where has that conger eel gone?

Smoked Fish, Apple & Beetroot

Serves 4

This dish can be made with either hot or cold smoked fish. I used some thin slices of cold smoked grey mullet that I prepared and smoked myself. Smoked eel, salmon or mackerel are equally suitable. I used some purslane and a couple of crisp Fiesta apples.

150–200g/6–8oz smoked fish
50g/2oz purslane
2 Fiesta apples
4 tbsps beetroot and horseradish chutney (see p. 186)
Olive oil
Black pepper
75ml/3fl oz lightly whipped double cream
Squeeze of lemon juice

If you are using cold smoked fish, use a sharp carving knife to thinly slice it. For hot smoked fish just pick it into large flakes.

Peel the apples and cut them into quarters, remove the core and then slice them.

Mix the lemon juice into the lightly whipped cream.

Dress the salad with a little olive oil.

Place the purslane on four plates, top with slices of apple, pieces of smoked fish and the beetroot and horseradish chutney and finally with the cream. Add a few twist of black pepper to finish.

Smoked Fish & Scrambled Egg

Serves 4

After my successful cold smoking of the dogfish, I decided to celebrate with a few slices to go with my scrambled eggs. You can, of course, use smoked salmon or any other cold smoked fish for this dish.

100g/4oz thinly sliced smoked fish
8 eggs
A little single cream or milk
Salt and black pepper
25g/1oz butter

Whisk the eggs in a bowl, with a little cream or milk. Season with salt and pepper.

Heat the butter in a saucepan and add the egg mix, cook gently, stirring continuously with a wooden spoon until it is scrambled.

Serve on warm toast and top with pieces of the smoked fish.

Tea Smoked Mackerel

This was an earlier effort at smoking fish. One day I nipped out and went down the road to buy some mackerel from the local fishermen. Mackerel is an excellent fish for smoking, as it is very oily and also very cheap, I remember paying 30 pence each for my four fish. My inspiration came when I was reminiscing about my time in Mongolia on horseback around the beautiful Lake Khosvgol. On the third day my guide, Gana, who indecently spoke two words of English, stopped to camp with some local fishermen in their settlement. Mongolians are not renowned for their cuisine, but these guys knew a thing or two about fishing, and how to smoke and preserve. How many fisherman do you know who fish with no bait? I was employed to gut fish as they flew out of the water. Happy memories.

They rubbed their fish with salt and then hung them on a wooden rack for a day. Then they would put them in their smoking pit and let them go... truly delicious when they first come out.

For my first attempt I decided to salt my fish for a few hours, rinse them off under cold water and pat them dry. Then I took a roasting tray and put a mixture of oak wood chippings, small pieces of coal and some green tea leaves. I then put this on the electric ring on a medium heat to start creating some smoke. I placed it over wire rack and then put the fish on. Then I covered it with some tin foil, reduced the heat to very low and just left the fish for a couple of hours.

They were delicious, and it inspired me to set about making a more permanent smoker.

Tea Smoked Mackerel
& Beetroot Sandwich

Serves 2

A delicious sandwich with two ingredients that are a cracking combination. You can of course use a normal smoked mackerel for this.

1 small tea smoked mackerel, skinned and flaked
1 tsp double cream
8 capers
Salt and black pepper
1 small beetroot, peeled and grated
4 thick slices of granary bread
Butter

Mix the mackerel with the cream, capers and seasoning.

Butter the slices of bread. Divide the mackerel mix equally, top with grated beetroot.

Sandwich together and enjoy.

Smoked Eel, Bacon & Mustard Potatoes

Serves 4

Given the choice I would choose smoked eel over salmon. Many people find eating eel a little off-putting, and it certainly does have a distinctive flavour that doesn't suit all palates. However, once smoked it becomes a significantly superior product. I'm sure if you can convince someone to try it they'll love it. I bought the eel from David at Deri-Mon Smokery in Dulas Bay, who catches them locally.

I used a Romano potato here and simply cut it into a large dice and gently boiled them, although a salad potato would be more suitable if you have them.

200g/8oz smoked eel fillet
4 pieces dry cured streaky bacon, rind removed
400g/1lb potatoes, cut into large dice
50ml/2fl oz olive oil
1 heaped tsp Dijon mustard
Salt and black pepper
Some salad leaves, I used purslane with mine

Cook the potatoes gently in lightly salted water. Drain well. Whisk together the olive oil and mustard and add to the potatoes, season with salt and pepper.

Grill the bacon until it is crispy.

Divide the eel into 4 portions and serve with the salad, potatoes and crispy bacon.

meat

A London Shepherd

I've always liked a challenge. I've ridden bicycles through the jungles of Zaire in Central Africa, ridden horses in Northern Mongolia, having never ridden before, and been through the Sahara desert in a two wheel drive van. However, when I first met Bini Jones and enthusiastically announced that I would like to get involved and help her on her farm, I didn't think she would get me to start immediately.

Well if you offer, you have to expect the offer to be accepted. She has a little job for me to do, and it involves the sheep up the hill, which she points out to me. A clue is offered when she presents me with a shepherd's crook and then tells me my job. She wants me to help her bring the sheep down from the field, back to the holding area by the house. At first I think she means all on my own – bloody hell, is she mad! Commercial suicide! My fears are put to rest, though, and she runs through what she wants me to do and some key points to remember.

All I have to do is walk in front of the sheep and guide them down the road back into the holding area. Bini will drive behind on her quad bike and steer them, cajoling them into some sort of order. Sounds simple, but with potential to be highly amusing.

One of the most important things for me to remember is that I must neither be too close nor too far from the sheep. Too close and they will run past me, too far ahead and they will not follow me. I must also walk at a constant, general pace in the middle of the road and stop ongoing traffic. Sounds fine, as long as there is no-one on the road who drives like me! The road we have to walk down is quite steep and windy, and so poses a few problems for the novice shepherd. Finally, if for any reason the sheep bolt pass me, I must stop them and get them under control.

The last point concerns me, making me feel quite nervous. I hope that dinner is not early tonight!

Bini sets off before me and I take the stroll up through the village, towards the gate that Bini has instructed me to wait at. The walk takes me about 10 minutes, and apart from a few funny looks from the locals, passes without incident.

I reach the gate – is it the right one, I can't see Bini anywhere? Then I hear some whistling and the purr and grinding of her quad bike. She's shouting instructions at her dog, and although I still can't see them, I'm confident I have the right gate. After about five minutes, the first of the sheep appear over the hill, Bini and her dog in hot pursuit! A few strays to gather up and then it will be my big moment. Bini reminds me of what she wants me to do, and tells me to set off down the road.

When I'm a little way down, she opens the gate and the sheep are off. Bini is immediately barking orders from the back and urging the sheep down the hill. She shouts to me to keep the pace and distance I'm at, and reminds me about on coming cars. I hear the first car coming, and prepare to push my crook forward into the air, achieving this with the confidence of an old hand. Another car, and again I stop it successfully. Bini continues to bark orders and the sheep appear to have taken a liking to a bank of grass on the right-hand side, so I stop briefly to wait. Have I done the right thing by stopping, just for a moment? I'm right, but then Bini shouts at me to move on. Another car and I'm beginning to relax a little, enjoying waving my stick at people and commanding them to stop. All this power, it's great!

Nearly in the village now, not far to go and all is well. We've just passed an old lady at the bus stop, who looks at me weirdly, smart lady! I shouted over to her, telling her it was my first day on the job, and it was going ok. My optimism was not to last long, for in my slightly relaxed state I hadn't noticed that one of the sheep had bolted and was just about to fly past me. Not good – there's a car coming towards me, another about to pull out at a junction, and I've got a loose sheep doing what the bloody hell he likes!

Where's the panic button? Bini is going to kill me and the old lady just started laughing at me!

Bini is screaming loudly now – time for action. I wave my stick at the car on the junction, which screeches to a halt. I now need to get the loose sheep under control. It's complete chaos, which seems to last forever, in reality it was all under control within a minute, although I'm not sure how much that was down to me. The drivers looked slightly annoyed – still, you can never have enough practice at emergency stops, so they should be thanking me really.

Bini tells me to move on. The gate we need to head towards enters Bini's property on a near blind corner, representing a final challenge. I hope the sheep follow me and don't decide to have a little run up around the corner. Bini urges me on as she keeps tight to the back, and the dog runs round to keep the livestock in check. I'm in, and they're following me! What a relief. Just the little stroll towards the holding field and job done. Some of the sheep go in without fuss, but a few feel like playing games, and we have one that is determined to get loose. We get him trapped by the house, but he makes a dash for it and Bini urges me to cut him off at the main gate to the field. I run to block him and urge him back towards the holding field. It seems to have worked and the dog does the rest. All in, and finally the job is done.

So how did I do? I feel that I messed up a little, and it was certainly harder then I expected – things can change in a split second, so you have to concentrate at all times. To my surprise, Bini congratulates me on a good first effort, and awards me a score of 6 out of 10. That's a lot more than I expected, so I'm really chuffed and feel quite pleased with my efforts. Wonder if she'll let me keep the crook?

Can't wait for my next job... spot of sheep shearing, perhaps?

Baked Shoulder Lamb, Mustard & Onions

Serves 6-8

1.4kg/3lb boned & rolled shoulder lamb
2 good tbsps English mustard
6 medium onions, peeled and cut in half
Large sprig rosemary
Salt and black pepper

Place the lamb in a bowl and use the mustard to cover the lamb. Season well with salt and black pepper.

Place the onions in a roasting tray and season with salt and pepper.

Place a sprig of rosemary on the onions and then place the lamb on top.

Cover with foil and then place in the oven at 160ºC/325ºF, gas mark 3 for about 3 hours.

Remove the foil for the last hour and baste the meat and onions a couple of times.

Remove from the oven and allow to rest for 20 minutes before carving.

Marinated Breast of Lamb Ribs

Serves 6

The breast of lamb is one of the least used cuts from a lamb carcass. Although it doesn't have a great deal of meat on, it is still tasty and if cooked correctly, will deliver a satisfying meal. It will give out a lot of fat during cooking, so it is very important to cook it on a rack in a roasting tray, to allow the fat to drain so the meat is not swimming in it.

You will usually see the breast boned and rolled, but when my lamb was being prepared I hit upon the idea of cutting them into small ribs and marinating them. You probably will not see them sold like this, so ask your butcher to prepare them for you.

1.5kg/3lbs breast of lamb ribs
2 tbsps natural yoghurt
1 tbsp honey
$^1/_2$ tsp ground cumin
1 tsp grated lemon zest
Salt and black pepper

Place the ribs in a large bowl and add the other ingredients. Mix everything together thoroughly.

Cover with cling film and place in the fridge for at least 4 hours. Place on a rack in a large roasting tray and cook in the oven at 160ºC/325ºF, gas mark 3 for 1/$^1/_2$ hours. You will need to turn them half way through cooking, so they colour evenly.

Chump of Lamb, Haricot Bean, Tomato & Red Wine Shallot Dressing

Serves 4

When a lamb is prepared by a butcher it produces two pieces of chump, and these will usually be cut immediately into chops. However, if the bone is removed and they are then cut into two across the grain of the meat, they produce excellent single portions that can be roasted and carved 'with the grain' into slices.

In restaurants this cut is very popular with chefs, and is generally known as the 'rump' on the menu. You'll probably have to ask your butcher to prepare this specially for you – just make sure you get there before he cuts all the chops.

2 chumps lamb, boned and cut into 4 mini joints
2 tbsp olive oil
150g/6oz chopped onion
2 crushed cloves garlic
200g/8oz cooked haricot beans
200g/8oz chopped tomatoes
1 tsp tomato paste
100ml/4fl oz water
Salt and pepper
12 black olives, pitted and cut in half
Small handful of torn basil leaves

4 tbsps red wine & shallot dressing (see below)

Heat the olive oil in a saucepan and add the onions. Cook these gently for about 10 minutes until soft. Add the garlic and cook for a few minutes.

Add the haricot beans, tomatoes, tomato paste, water and seasoning. Mix together, cover with a lid and simmer gently for 25–30 minutes.

Meanwhile, heat a heavy bottomed frying pan. When it is very hot, add the lamb chumps fat side down and quickly brown them. There is no need to add any oil, the fat on the lamb will be sufficient.

Transfer to a roasting tray, season with salt and pepper and cook in an oven at 200°C/400°F, gas mark 6 for about 12 minutes. This will make your lamb pink. Remove from the pan and allow to rest for at least 5 minutes.

Finish the beans by adding the olives and basil.

Carve the lamb and serve with beans and the red wine and shallot dressing.

Red Wine Shallot Dressing

In a pan put four finely chopped shallots with 200ml/8fl oz red wine and boil until you have about a tablespoon of liquid left.

Place the reduction in a bowl, add 100ml/4fl oz red wine vinegar and half a teaspoon of Dijon style mustard. Whisk in 300ml/12fl oz olive oil and season with salt and pepper.

Store in a bottle and use as required.

Grilled Lamb Cutlets & Green Sauce

Serves 4

The green sauce is loosely based around the Italian sauce called salsa verde, made in a similar way but with parsley, basil and mint instead of the salad leaves. I cooked this in February and herbs were in short supply, but I saw some bags of mixed leaves in Hooton's and so put them to good use. This recipe makes too much sauce for 4, but will keep well in the fridge for a week. Good with grilled fish, pork, chicken and beef.

Green Sauce
100g/4oz mixed rocket, mizuna & red mustard
1 tbsp mint leaves
1 clove garlic
$^1/_2$ tsp Dijon mustard
3 heaped tsps capers and a tsp of liquor from jar
200ml/9fl oz olive oil
1 tsp red wine vinegar

Salt and black pepper
8–12 lamb cutlets

Place the mixed leaves, mint and garlic in a food processor and blend until they are quite fine. Add the mustard, capers, olive oil, red wine vinegar and seasoning. Blend to combine.

Heat a ribbed skillet pan and brush lightly with oil. Season the cutlets with salt and pepper and place them in the pan, cook over a medium heat for about 3 minutes each side (this cooks them pink – if you want it well done, cook for about 5 minutes a side).

Let the cutlets rest for about 3–4 minutes. Serve with some of the green sauce.

Generation Game

How many of us can say we have followed in our father's footsteps, continued a family tradition and made the old man proud? I certainly never had any intention of becoming a painter and decorator like my dad, not because I didn't respect what he did – indeed as a kid I used to love helping him in my school holidays. He is retired now, but in his profession he was highly skilled, loyal to his clients and could turn his hand to many of the finer points of the craft, including gold leaf sign writing. Me, well I was going to be a top football player, earn loads of money and be on the back page of *The Sun*. Then reality strikes and you have decisions to make, so I became a chef. Not exactly a family tradition, though my father tells me that my great grandmother was a great cook, and served in a big house in Gloucestshire.

Brian Thomas followed in his father's footsteps, a tradition that has been in his family for five generations. They have farmed in the same part of Anglesey for all that time, through thick and thin – BSE, foot and mouth, intensive farming – so tradition is very important. Brian and his wife, Fiona, run Beef Direct from their farm in Llannerch-y-medd, where they farm pedigree Welsh Blacks, Welsh Black mountain lamb, Suffolk Lamb, and have recently started raising pigs. One look at the field by their house and you would know there were pigs around – it is February, and they've had a lot of rain and the paddock is a complete shambles!

It's beef with which they originally made their name, and the foundation of their business. Fiona, a school teacher by profession, deals with all the administrative side, including marketing, although she confesses this is mostly by word of mouth. This leaves Brian to run the farm and deal with the butchers he employs to prepare his meat, make sausages, burgers etc.

Brian's family have kept Welsh Blacks since 1930, and he's very passionate about them, believing them to be an animal that produces some of the best beef in the British Isles. His father bred the famous bull Chwaen Major 15th, which won all the major and many interbreed championships. He also claims that the land in Anglesey contributes to the meat's superior nature – the pastures here are rich in clover, and this all adds to the flavour in the end product. He calls it "good fattening land" or "good finishing land", and perhaps this is why there is such history of quality beef on Anglesey. They produce well marbled, flavoured, textured and succulent beef, and his customers certainly seem to agree, especially one who felt obliged to ring them on Boxing Day one year to congratulate them on the quality! Brian remembers selling them a large rib of his Welsh Black, which he had hung for three weeks. What he didn't know was that they left it in the fridge for another four weeks, and said it was the best they had ever tasted! Rich!

Although they sell directly from Anglesey, they don't have a farm shop – their main market is the ever growing farmers' markets. They attend six monthly markets, and Brian was careful to select those that he thought would bring him the most success. It seems to have worked brilliantly. They attend markets in Altrincham, Liverpool (twice), New Ferry Wirral, Wrexham and Ashton-under-Lyne. They began the markets about five years ago, at a time, when Brian confesses to being frustrated with the way things were going. He wanted to take more control of his destiny, meet the public face-to-face, tell them how good his meat was and make things work better financially. When he first started the markets he had plenty of time to talk with the customers, tell them how he reared the animals, all about the breed, the hanging process, and so on. Now, he's so busy that it's job enough to keep the queues to a minimum.

He seems really happy with the way the public have responded. He has a very loyal customer base, and even if some stray, they soon come back because they can't get the quality of his meat – once tasted, you can't go back to mediocre meat. He is very passionate about the traditional breeds of the British Isles, the quality meat they produce, which he says is world class. He is extremely critical of the European breeds that seem to be all the rage in the commercial world, where speed and size are the main factors. Most of them, he says, come from dairy herds, and you just can't produce the same quality – no character and no flavour.

Their livestock is certified organic, and they use only local abattoirs,lthough since the closure of Caenarfon, they have had to travel a little further to Colwyn Bay and Conway Meats. They offer great value for money, and for what you get, their meat is reasonably priced. In fact, on my way back from Anglesey I decided to pop into the Co-op in Pwllheli and see how much their organic beef was. It might surprise you but their sirloin steaks were priced at £17.05 a kilo – Brian's steaks will set you back only £13.70 a kilo, and let me tell you there is no competition, no competition at all.

Their success, although great, has brought them a dilemma, and with it a decision on their future direction. They are so busy that they are struggling to keep up with demand, and are thinking about possibly increasing the size of their operation.

Whatever they decide, I'm sure you can rely on several things remaining the same. The quality of their beef, the consistently top grade service, and a belief that maintaining traditions will see them through whatever challenges lie ahead.

Anglesey Lamb & Barley

Serves 4-6

For this dish I used some neck of lamb, a few pieces of breast and some bones from the best end. Use all neck if you wish, or you can also use chump chops or good pieces of breast. You will need to chop the carrots, swede and potatoes into a large pieces for this hearty, simple dish. Best eaten in bowls and served with warm, crusty bread.

1 tbsp vegetable oil
200g/9oz sliced onion
200g/9oz chopped carrots
200g/9oz chopped swede
700g/1lb 12oz neck of lamb
2–4 cloves chopped garlic
Good sprig of rosemary
1 litre/2 pints water
Salt and black pepper
100g/4oz pearl barley
200g/9oz chopped potatoes

Heat a saucepan or flameproof casserole dish. Add the oil and onions and cook over a gentle heat for 10 minutes, until slightly softened. Add the carrots and swede and cook for 5 minutes.

Place the lamb on top of the vegetables and add the garlic, rosemary, water and salt and pepper. Bring slowly to the boil and skim any fat that rises to the top. Cover with a lid and simmer very gently for 1 1/2 hours. Add the pearl barley and potatoes to the pot and stir into the stew.

Cover with the lid and continue to cook for about 30 minutes or until the potatoes and barley are cooked.

Stuffed Loin of Lamb

Serves 2-4

When I had my whole lamb prepared, I had the saddle split into two lengthways and both pieces were then chined. You will usually see the loin cut into chops, which is a shame as it is ideal for this dish. If you are not confident of preparing the lamb for stuffing, I'm sure you can ask your butcher to do it. I love prunes with lamb, so they form part of the simple stuffing for this dish.

600g/1lb 4oz loin of lamb, chined
6 pitted prunes, cut into 4
1 tbsp roughly chopped parsley
1 tbsp coarse white breadcrumbs
1 tbsp olive oil
Salt and black pepper

Lay the loin of lamb on a chopping board and roll out the flap. The meat should be on top, and you will see a small, thin piece of meat attached to it, remove this and leave to one side.

Place the lamb between two pieces of cling film, and with a rolling pin or meat hammer start hitting the flap to flatten it slightly. It needs to be long enough to wrap completely around the lamb. Remove the top layer of cling film.

Take the smaller piece of meat and place it between 2 pieces of cling film and lightly bat it out to flatten it slightly.

In a bowl mix up the prunes, parsley, breadcrumbs, olive oil and seasoning.

Lay the stuffing on to the main piece of lamb and spread evenly.

Place the smaller piece of lamb on top.

Using the cling film, roll the lamb up. Place in the fridge for an hour.

Remove the cling film and tie the lamb with 4 pieces of string.

Heat a frying pan and seal the lamb all over until brown. Transfer to a small roasting tray, season with salt and black pepper and cook in an oven at 200oc/400of, gas mark 6 for 20 minutes for pink, 25 minutes for medium and 30-35 for well done.

Allow to rest for at least 10 minutes before carving.

Lamb's Liver, Mustard Mash & Onions

Serves 4

When cooked sympathetically, lamb's liver is excellent and should be eaten a lot more. The important thing is to cook it for a short time and leave it nice and pink in the middle.

The mustard mash here, uses the strong English mustard and adds a good heat to the creamy potatoes.

8 slices lambs liver
750g/1lb 14oz potatoes
125ml/5fl oz milk
25g/1oz butter
1 1/2 tsps/2tsp English mustard
Salt and pepper
4 portions of braised onions

Peel and cut the potatoes into even sized pieces. Place them in a saucepan and pour in enough cold water to cover, add some salt. Place on the heat and bring to the boil. Reduce the heat and cover with a lid and simmer until the potatoes are just cooked. Drain and then mash.

Heat the milk and butter until the butter is melted. Pour onto the potatoes, add the mustard and seasoning. Mix together and beat well with a wooden spoon.

Heat a frying pan and add a good knob of butter and a touch of oil. Season the lambs liver and cook over a medium-hot heat for about 1 1/2 minutes each side or until it is pink.

Serve with the mustard mash and braised onions.

Lamb & Chickpeas

Serves 4

3 tbsps olive oil
200g/8oz chopped onion
1 tsp ground cumin
Pinch of saffron
500g/ 1lb 4oz diced neck fillet lamb
4 cloves chopped garlic
1 tbsp tomato puree
400g/ 14oz chopped tomatoes
200g/8oz chickpeas, soaked & drained
500ml/20fl oz water
1 strip of lemon peel
Salt & black pepper

Heat the olive oil in a heavy saucepan and add the onions. Cook over a gentle heat for about 10 minutes, or until a little soft.

Add the cumin and saffron and cook for 3 minutes, to allow the spices to cook.

Add the lamb and garlic and mix into the onions. Cook for about 5 minutes over a medium heat.

Add the tomato paste, chickpeas, chopped tomatoes, water, lemon peel and seasoning.

Bring to the boil, then reduce the heat, cover with a lid and then simmer very gently for about 1 hour 40 minutes.

Foil Roasted Porthmadog Salt Marsh Lamb

Serves 4–6

On the road into Porthmadog, if you look to the right you will see many sheep grazing on the salt marshes. There are many such areas all over the country, and it produces a light, delicate meat that has a subtle, natural saltiness. You can buy it in these parts from local butchers between May and September, just look out for the signs outside the shop fronts.

If you don't like the hassle of basting meat then this recipe is right up your street. Also by wrapping it in foil, all the flavours are sealed in and they permeate the meat. Speed is not everything, and slower cooking of meat really is good, producing soft, succulent flesh. The flavours used here are very traditional – don't be scared off by the amount of garlic, as it will enhance not overpower, becoming more mellow the longer it is cooked.

$^1/_2$ leg lamb (approx 1kg/2lb8oz)
1 head garlic
4 large sprigs rosemary
Anglesey sea salt
Crushed black pepper

Score/slash the lamb with a sharp knife. Stuff with pieces of garlic and sprigs of rosemary.

Season well and wrap tightly in foil.

Bake in the oven for about 3 hours on 160ºC/325ºF, gas mark 3. Peel back the foil for the last 40 minutes of cooking to allow the top to colour slightly.

Grilled Onglet of Beef, Parsley & Garlic Butter

Serves 4

One of the most flavoursome steaks you can eat, although great care needs to be taken in cooking and slicing the meat. The onglet hangs between the last rib and the loin, and is quite a grainy cut of beef. It is important to cook it rare, over a fierce heat, and then allow it to rest for 5–10 minutes. You then need a very sharp carving knife to slice against the grain. If you slice with the grain, you'll be chewing it all day. Once you've tried it, you will be converted to its delicious flavour. You can also use skirt and thin flank for this dish. Serve it with some home-made chips.

500g/1lb 4oz onglet of beef
A little oil for frying
125g/5oz butter, slightly softened
25g/1oz flat leaf parsley, finely chopped
2 cloves garlic
5 twists black pepper

Mix the butter with the flat leaf parsley, garlic and black pepper. Place in a piece of cling film and then roll it into a sausage shape. If you are not using it immediately you can keep it in the fridge or in the freezer.
Heat a large heavy griddle pan or frying pan. Brush the piece of beef with oil and then season with salt and black pepper. Cook over a medium-high heat for about 3–4 minutes a side.
Allow to rest for at least 5 minutes.

Melt a generous amount of the garlic and parsley butter. Carve the steak across the grain in to thin slices.

Pour over some butter and serve with chunky home-made chips.

Cottage Pie

Serves 6

Simple, delicious comfort food. Traditionally made with leftover cooked beef, it has become slightly refined over the years. As Jane Grigson noted in *English Food*, anyone can cook steak but the real skill of a cook is to take modest fayre and turn it into something special. A great dish to stick in the middle of the table, served with some steaming green vegetables.

The Worcestershire sauce is a must in this.

1 tbsp vegetable oil
1 medium onion, finely chopped
2 medium carrots, peeled and diced
700g/1lb 12oz minced beef
2 cloves garlic, crushed
100g/4oz chopped leek
2 dessert spoons plain flour
2 dessert spoons tomato puree
1 bay leaf
1 tsp chopped thyme
Salt and black pepper
Good splash of Worcestershire sauce
500ml/20fl oz beef stock

1kg/2lb 8oz floury potatoes
50ml/2fl oz milk
50g/2oz butter
Salt and pepper
50g/2oz grated cheddar cheese

Cook the onion and carrots in the oil until they start to soften.

Increase the heat and add the beef mince, fry until it is well broken up and lightly brown.

Add the garlic, leek and cook for 2–3 minutes over a medium heat.

Add the flour, tomato paste, bay leaf, thyme. Stir well.

Season well with salt and black pepper.

Add the beef stock and Worcestershire sauce and simmer for 15 minutes.

Boil the potatoes, drain and mash. Add the butter, milk salt and pepper.

Pour the beef into a suitable ovenproof dish and top with the potato and grated cheese.

Bake for 1 hour at 190ºC/375ºF gas mark 5.

Slipping & Sliding

Sometimes when you set out on a journey, however long or small, you can expect certain situations to arise, certain problems that you must face. Planning, I feel, is a most sophisticated word, and one that is well beyond my reach sometimes. However, it can prevent you from getting into many sticky situations, and help your journey go smoothly. Hell, where's the fun in that?! Problems are there to be faced, and you can only do that when you know what they are.

All week in Aberdaron they had been expecting some snow, which I'm reliably informed by Mr Jones the baker, is a rare thing in this little oasis by the sea. In fact, the last time they had any serious snow here, was in 1982. It was that bad that some people got stuck here for a week and had to spend the whole time in the Ship Inn... tough life being stuck in the pub all day, especially if you are on the wagon. Today is no different, not a spot of white to be seen, and no sign on the surrounding hills. So as I set out in my little Nissan, reversed out of the drive and up the track and onto the road, little did I know the adventure that lay ahead.

Today I'm off to visit Gwyn Thomas, who farms in the Ogwen Valley, nestled between the mountains of Snowdonia, a few miles outside Bethesda. I'd been here before, towards the end of last summer, when I stayed at the hostel, nestled in the valley at Capel Cruig.

The journey should have taken me about an hour, through Pwllehi, head towards Caenarfon and then cut on to Telford's A5, through Bethesda and on to Capel Cruig. The usual road works out of Abedarron, it seems the broadband revolution is coming to town, so the whole place is being ripped to shreds before the tourist season kicks in at Easter. Through Pwllehi, onto the A499, drive for about 20 minutes and then a quick glance to my right and the snow topped peaks of Snowdonia are in my sights. A few flakes of snow start to fall on the screen. By the time I get on to the A5, the snow is coming down really heavily and the conditions don't look like improving.

I reach the turning for the hostel and notice a couple of mountain rescue vehicles next door. It's at this point I should have realised that things were not shaping up for the Nissan and me. As you pass the hostel, you enter onto a track that leads you round the valley. Not usually a problem, but today it is covered in snow. Fortunately people have been driving this way, so there are well defined tracks. After a couple of minutes I pass a four wheel drive jeep, that is pulled over on the side, chuck them all a little wave and a smile and move on. No problems so far, no slopes or ice to deal with, and the little motor is making light work of it all. A few gentle slopes appear and we negotiate them quite successfully, although I hadn't actually noticed that we were quite high now and the drops down the hill on my right-hand side were becoming bigger.

At this point I started to get a little concerned with my foolhardy approach, and notice a little further up that the small fences that act like a barrier had suddenly disappeared. El Problemo! I also see that there are several more severe slopes to be negotiated and some patches of ice are appearing. It is now very important to keep a steady momentum going, employ first gear and take it very gently. Now I think being slightly scared in these situations helps you a little, it helps you to respect the fact that you are in a bit of trouble and makes you concentrate all your energies on the task. What definitely doesn't do you any favours is panicking – oh, and using the brakes is included in that. For this reason I am glad to be on my own, no-one there to tell you the obvious things like "be careful that's a big drop" or "we're sliding, do something"... and most importantly, no shouting.

The snow is becoming heavier by now, and it's coming straight at the car, making visibility a bit of a problem. In what seems about 10 minutes, but was actually seconds, the car seems to be sliding all over the place, and I come close to the edge on more than one occasion. Fortunately I can see the fence starting again soon, and this gives me a little boost. Also, I seem to be over the steepest parts now, and I can see that what lies ahead is a lot flatter. I drive on and it suddenly occurs to me that I've forgotten where Gwyn says his house is, so I decide to stop at the house I can see at the bottom and ask for directions. A slightly startled lady answers the door and I ask where Gwyn lives. "Ooh, back up there." I hope she's bloody joking. I'm not going back up there. She asks me which way I have come, and when I tell her her answer is "Are you mad?" Well yes, probably. And then "Well done for making it." Why thanks very much, I think.

She tells me not to attempt going back that way, but to park in Gwen's yard at the bottom and then walk up. I jump in the car and reverse, turn around and then see that jeep approaching, who pulls over to let me go, only I can't because the wheels are not gripping, so I'm playing a kind of keep fit treadmill car game. I whack it into reverse and go back a little, stop, back into first and drive gently on by. I pass a man walking his dog, who I later discover is Gwyn, and then proceed to miss the turning – great. I end up having to reverse down a slight slope for about 100 metres to join the track I should be on. Finally, my destination is in sight, although I'm slightly concerned that the person I'm meeting is going in the opposite direction... hope he won't be long.

I park the car and amble up the side to the house. His wife Nia answers the door and tells me he's gone to walk the dog, and could be about and hour. To be fair I am about 40 minutes late, but this time at least I've a good excuse. She grabs her binoculars, but just as she says I might like to drive down to see if I can catch him, she spots him, so I decide to walk down and meet him.

Gwyn has been farming here for the last 10 years, and comes from a proud tradition of farming stock. His family have been raising sheep and cattle for five generations, and you can immediately tell his fierce devotion and passion to it.

He keeps pure bred Welsh Blacks here and Welsh Mountain

sheep. When he first took over the farm he had about 1200 sheep, but in the first year he cut this to 600 and in the second to 300. This seemed a little strange to me, but he explained that this was a suitable number for this type of terrain and ensured that nature's resources were enough to maintain them.

When you think of farmers, perhaps you see them milking cows, shearing sheep or mucking out the sheds. Of course you are right, but they are a lot more than that. They are guardians of the land, they respect their surroundings and help to maintain and protect the fine balance between nature and our use of it. Gwyn is part of a scheme called Tir Gofal which is an all-Wales Agri-Environment Scheme, administered by the Countryside Council for Wales. It aims to encourage agricultural practices that will protect and enhance the landscapes, their cultural features and associated wildlife. It incorporates a basic 'Whole Farm Section' comprising minimum environmental requirements for the entire holding. It also involves managing existing wildlife habitats in accordance with certain guidelines. One of the main reasons for keeping fewer sheep is to allow heather regeneration on the mountain. The re-building of walls is also included in the agreement. This is the common sense approach to farming, and one that Gwyn is justly proud of.

Tradition seems extremely important to him, and he says the way he is farming now is similar in many ways to the ways of the 1700s. All of the feed is supplied from his own farm – he grows swedes to sustain the animals through the winter. The sheep spend the winter in Bridge North, where there is grass all year round, and then from mid-march Gwyn leaves his Ogwen Valley home to be with the sheep at a very important and crucial time for him. When we are chatting about this, it reminds me of the nomads of Mongolia, who travel to find the best conditions and pasture for their animals.

When he is away, Nia – who for most of the year works as a nurse – takes over the farm. She normally takes two weeks from her holiday allowance, and then the rest she manages in the evenings.

In their early days they used to run a B&B for visitors, which helped them pay back money from a bank loan. Gwyn's grandparents also used to do this in the 1930s, when things were significantly different. In those days it would be cyclists and people travelling by train who would visit. They would stay for the weekend and eat with the family at meal times. Gwyn feels there was a greater understanding of country folk then, which he says is sadly lacking these days. He would like to see this reversed, and feels everyone would benefit, one of the reasons he believes passionately in the nature trail he set up. If he can educate a few of the people that visit on the importance of caring for the environment he farms, then he says it is a success. He has over 3000 visitors a year here, and this area gets some half a million.

He enjoys showing people the conditions in which his animals thrive, explaining why they suit this terrain. Welsh Mountain sheep thrive on poor pasture, and are very tough and adaptable. They are bred for these conditions and produce good meat.

He has two outlets for his meat – he supplies Tesco and Waitrose with about 350 lambs for their Welsh organic lamb. Those for Tesco have to travel to Merthyr Tydfil, a distance of 170 miles. Gwyn is clearly unhappy about this, though of course he has no choice, but would prefer to have his animals slaughtered locally, so it is less stressful for them. His other outlet is selling direct from his farm and mail order to customers all over the country. This has proved very successful, and sometimes he has a problem keeping up with demand. Financially it is more profitable to sell direct, although as he points out, it takes a lot more time. At the moment he is happy with the balance.

Gwyn certainly seems to know where he is going and offers the public a real insight into what he does and the importance of the countryside and the correct management of it.

He also knows that he isn't going to walk down to the yard with me to my car – it is still snowing heavily as I leave!

Beef, Beer & Onions

Serves 4

A really simple, tasty, gutsy dish. Minimum ingredients equals maximum flavour here, and you could easily make this into a pie if you wish. Gwyn Thomas kindly sent me away with a few bits of beef after I visited him. A reward for making it along the snowy mountain pass to his house in my little Nissan.

25g/1oz beef dripping
800g/1 1/2 lbs diced stewing beef
Flour for dusting
450g/1lb 2oz sliced onions
250ml/10fl oz dark beer
250ml/10fl oz beef stock
Few splashes of Worcestershire sauce
Salt and black pepper

Heat a large flameproof casserole dish with the dripping. Dust the meat with some flour and fry to lightly brown it all. Remove from the pan and leave to one side.

Reduce the heat and add the onions, cover with a lid and cook gently for about 15 minutes until soft.

Add the beef back to the pot and pour in the beer, stock and a few splashes of Worcestershire sauce. Season well with salt and pepper and place on a lid. You can either simmer very gently on top of the stove for 2 1/2 hours or place in the oven at 160°C/325°F, gas mark 3 for the same amount of time.

Rump Steak & Mushrooms

Serves 2

A very tasty cut of steak, can be a little tougher if cut from nearer the topside and not the neatest thing to portion either. Still, sometimes you need your teeth to work a little harder.

Always rest your steak after cooking for at least 5 minutes, allowing the juices to settle and the proteins to relax. Always season your meat just before hitting the pan or just after cooking if you prefer. The mushrooms for this I picked at Jill and Mikes', they were leaning up against their back door!

2 x 175g/7oz rump steaks
25g/1oz butter
1 tbsp vegetable oil
4–5 shitake mushrooms, sliced
4–5 oyster mushrooms, sliced
Few drops Worcestershire sauce
1 clove garlic, crushed
2 small shallots, peeled and sliced
1 dessert spoon chopped parsley

Heat the butter and oil in frying pan.

Season the steaks with sea salt and cracked black pepper.

Place the steaks in the pan and cook, over a medium heat for 2 minutes each side for rare, 3 minutes for medium and 5 minutes each side for well done.

Remove the steaks from the pan and allow to rest.

Add the shallots and cook gently for 4–5 minutes until slightly softened.

Add the garlic and mushrooms and saute for 5 minutes. Season with a few drops of Worcestershire sauce or to your taste.

Add the parsley and serve with the steaks.

Steak, Red Wine & Shallots

Serves 4

A very simple dish that you can make with rump, sirloin, rib-eye or fillet steak. I used rump when I made this, which I got from E.T. Jones in Bodedern on Anglesey. The most important thing about this dish is to make sure the shallots are really soft and lightly caramelised to bring out their sweetness, which balances well with the red wine.

4 x 200g/8oz steaks
50g/2oz butter
200g/8oz chopped shallot
200ml/8fl oz red wine
Salt and pepper

Melt half the butter in a small pan and cook the shallots for about 10–15 minutes over a gentle heat, covered with a lid. When they are soft, add the wine and reduce by about half.

Whisk in the remaining butter and season with salt and pepper. Grill or pan fry the steaks to your liking. Allow to rest for 5 minutes and add any of the juices to the sauce.

Bring the sauce back to the boil, check the consistency and serve with the steaks.

Steak Sandwich with Red Onion Chutney

Serves 2

I had a sirloin steak that Gwyn Thomas gave me when I visited him, so I decided to make these sandwiches. You can use pieces of rump, rib-eye, fillet or minute steaks, it doesn't really matter, they will all produce a good eat. A good one to use the red onion chutney with.

200g/8oz sirloin steak
2 dessert spoons red onion chutney (see p. 187)
Handful of leaves (rocket, mizuna, red mustard)
Salt and black pepper
4 thick slices of white bread
Butter

Slice the steak in half lengthways and then in half again. Alternatively, you can grill the steak whole and slice it after cooking.

Season the steak and grill quickly in a ribbed skillet pan or fry quickly in a frying pan.

Toast the bread and spread with a little butter.

Spread the red onion chutney on the toast, top with steak and a few leaves.

Back to Basics,
Back to Tradition

When you hear the term 'rare' you suddenly think, endangered, shouldn't touch that, let alone eat it. It makes me think of rare animals in the world like the great mountain gorillas in Africa, Irwaady fresh water dolphins of the Mekong river, the white rhino in Africa...

In the case of our traditional breeds of meat in this country, the opposite is true. By openly encouraging people to eat them we place their very survival as a commitment to their numbers growing in our country.

In these times of mass production, where size of animal dictates the price, the speed with which it grows or is encouraged to, it is heartening to know that there are farmers prepared to buck the trend and produce animals of real quality. Reared by traditional methods on natural diets – no growth promoters, hormones or the routinely fed antibiotics – these animals are all full bred and true to the traditional stock. Like you and I, they are very adaptable to their surroundings, often hardy and slow to mature by nature.

For the cook these traditional breeds offer a diversion from mediocrity, and instead offer meat of character and distinction. All breeds have very different qualities, rather like different apples, grapes that produce wine and potatoes that are best for certain cooking methods. Anyone who has tasted beef from Dexter, pork from Tamworth pigs or lamb from Dorset Down will happily tell you so. The fat levels in the meat can sometimes be higher than modern cross bred animals, which on first reflection might suggest it is unhealthy. However, this has recently been disproved by scientists. They found that animals reared in a traditional way on only grass carry higher proportions of polyunsaturated fats that do not affect the body's cholesterol levels.

There are credited butchers across the country who have been picked for their skill at handling the meat. Correct hanging increases not only the flavour but the succulence of meat. Have a look at the marbling on a piece of beef from pure bred Welsh Black and the creamy fat on the joint, correctly reared and correctly cared for throughout the whole process. One look and taste of this and you will think twice about returning to that light red meat, nice and neatly packaged on the shelves of your standard supermarket.

I once had meat from a White Park animal that was delicious, a little gamey and very lean, every mouthful a taste sensation. Better to eat a little decent meat than a large quantity of mediocre meat.

Look out for the RBST (Rare Breeds Survival Trust) symbol at butchers, and you can be sure of the highest standards of preparation. All the meat comes from small farms where the farmers have the highest standards of animal welfare – they don't farm intensively, and the animals live in a stress-free environment. These animal will have full traceability, which reassures you of the provenance of the meat you are about to eat.

Get back to basics – you are what you eat, so it is important to know what they have been eating. Bring back the tradition!

Honey Pork, Apples & Root Vegetables

Serves 4-6

I like to use a nice fatty piece of belly pork for this, it stands up well to a slow, long cook. However, a lot of the belly pork sold commercially is so lean and has little fat. Sadly, this misses the point of this cut, and indeed other cuts of pork. The fat gives great flavour and helps keep the meat from drying out, and so remaining really succulent. In this dish the fat and juices will also help to add flavour to the vegetables.

I used Crown Gold apples in this recipe and some delicious honey from P J Haywood in Edern. The honey is added towards the end of cooking, and the meat basted several times, so it is left with a good, sticky glaze.

1 kg/2lb 8oz piece of belly pork
1 medium beetroot, cut into wedges
2 parsnips, cut lengthways and into large chunks
2 carrots, cut lengthways and into large chunks
1 medium red onion, cut into wedges
1 small swede, cut in half, then into slices
$^1/_2$ head garlic
2 sprigs of rosemary
Olive oil or vegetable oil
2 Crown Gold apples, cut in half and core removed
Welsh Wildflower honey

Bring a pan of water to the boil and blanch the vegetables for five minutes and drain well.

Score the top of the pork with a sharp knife and rub some sea salt into it.

Place all the vegetables in a large roasting tray, add the garlic and the rosemary. Pour over a little oil and add some seasoning, mix together.

Place the pork on the top and cover with tin foil.

Place in an oven at 180°C/350°F, gas mark 4 for about 45 minutes, then remove the foil and add the apples.

Cook for a further 1 hour and then remove the pork. Let it cool slightly, then carefully take off the skin.

Place the pork back in the roasting tray and spoon over a dessert spoon of honey. Either put the skin to the side of the pork to crisp or on a separate tray. Put it back in the oven and cook for a further 30 minutes, basting a couple of times to glaze the pork.

Serve the pork sliced with some crackling, veg, apples and any juices from the pan.

Jellied Ham & Parsley

Serves 4

Ham hocks or shanks really should be used much more by cooks. Firstly it is incredibly inexpensive, very tasty and can be used in a great many things. Long slow cooking is what is required here, slow poaching in liquid will not only give you delicious soft meat but a great stock to make soup from. This dish is prepared in much the same way as brawn, the classic preparation using pig's head – you can by all means have a go at that, if you can get hold of a pig's head. Just don't ask in your local supermarket!

This is great served with a soft boiled egg on the side and maybe a few capers.

1 shank or hock of dry cured ham, soaked overnight in water
1 medium onion, cut in half
$^1/_2$ a leek
4 cloves garlic
1 carrot peeled
8 black peppercorns
A few parsley stalks, a little thyme and a bay leaf

Drain the soaked ham shank.

Place in a suitable pot and cover with cold water.

Add the remaining ingredients to the pot. Bring to the boil, skim off any scum that rises to the surface. Cover with a lid and reduce the heat and simmer very gently for about 2–2$^1/_2$ hours, or until the meat is really soft. It should just fall off the bone and offer no resistance.

Allow the hock to cool slightly in the stock.

Soak 2 leaves of gelatin in a bowl of cold water.

Take 1 litre/2 pints of the stock and place in a saucepan. Bring to the boil and reduce so you have 500ml/1 pint left.

Take the gelatin from the water and gently squeeze it. Then add it to the hot stock and whisk thoroughly. Leave to cool slightly.

Remove all the meat from the shank and tear it into a bowl.

Add 30g/1 1/4oz roughly chopped flat leaf parsley, season with a little salt and black pepper and pour in the cooled stock mix. Mix thoroughly.

Place the mix in a suitable bowl. Cover with cling film.

Place in the refrigerator and it will be ready to use within a few hours.

Gammon, Fried Egg & Mustard

Serves 4

I used duck eggs for this recipe, bought from Mr Jones the baker in Aberdaron.

4 x gammon steaks
4 free range duck eggs
2 heaped tsps grain mustard
40g/ 1³/₄oz butter
Some roughly chopped flat leaf parsley
Salt and black pepper
A liitle vegetable oil for frying eggs

Grill the gammon steaks on both sides.

Fry the eggs.

Heat a small pan and add the butter, cook until it is a light, nutty brown in colour. Add the mustard and parsley, stir in well.

Serve with the gammon and eggs.

Bacon, Bean & Cabbage Soup

Serves 4–6

Pulses are a great thing to cook with – cheap, nutritious and interesting. The haricot beans must be well cooked in this recipe, no bite at all or they are inedible and upset the soup. This is a really substantial, tasty soup, great with cheesy croutons on top.

100g/4oz haricot beans, soaked in cold water overnight
1 tbsp olive oil
1 medium onion, finely chopped
2 medium carrots, peeled and diced
2 clove garlic, sliced thinly
100g/4oz diced cooked bacon
400g/1lb chopped fresh tomatoes
1 litre/ 1 1/2 pints vegetable stock or water
200g/8oz chopped pointed cabbage, washed and drained
Salt and pepper

Drain the beans, place them in a pan and cover with cold water. Bring to the boil, skim off any scum that rises to the surface. Then simmer gently for 45–50 minutes, or until the beans are well cooked and the skin is not tough. This can be done in advance. Heat the olive oil in a separate pan, add the onion and carrots and coat with the oil. Cover with a lid and gently sweat for about 15 minutes, or until the onions are nice and soft. Add the bacon, stir in and cook for another 10 minutes with the lid on.

Add the tomatoes and garlic, cook over a high heat for 5 minutes. Add the stock, cooked haricot beans, salt and pepper and bring to the boil. Simmer gently for about 20 minutes. Add the chopped cabbage and stir into soup, cook gently, covered with a lid for 5 minutes.

Smoked Sausages & Baked Beans

Serves 4

I got some great smoked pork sausages from Deri-Mon smokery on Anglesey and decided to create a real comfort eating dish. Lots of us love baked beans, I sure do, so I've used haricot beans and flavored them with tomatoes and oregano. Baked slowly, it allows the beans to soften and just begin to split slightly, which is perfect for this. If you can't find smoked sausages, you can substitute with a good plain or spiced pork sausage.

200g/8oz haricot beans, soaked in water overnight
2 tbsps olive oil
8 smoked sausages
200g/8oz chopped onion
100g/4oz diced carrot
4 crushed cloves garlic
400g/1lb chopped tomatoes
1 tbsp tomato paste
1 tsp dried oregano
Salt and black pepper
350ml/13fl oz chicken stock

Drain the haricot beans. Heat the olive oil and add the sausages and brown lightly on both sides. Add the onions and carrot, reduce the heat slightly and cook gently for about 10 minutes, turning the ingredients occasionally. Add the garlic, tomatoes and tomato paste, bring to the boil and cook until the tomatoes have broken down a little. Add the haricot beans, oregano, salt and pepper and the stock. Bring to the boil, then cover with a lid or tin foil.

Place in the oven at 160ºC/325ºF, gas mark 3 for about 2 hours.

Bodedern Pâté

When I went to visit Ifan Jones at his butchers in Bodedern, I bought several things, among them a piece of belly pork and some pig's liver. Perfect for this rustic pâté, which is based on the French 'Pâté de Campagne'

1kg/2lb 8oz diced belly pork
500g/1lb 4oz sliced pigs liver
75g/3oz finely chopped shallots
2 crushed cloves garlic
100g/4oz chopped prunes
50ml/2fl oz brandy
Zest of $^1/_2$ orange and $^1/_4$ lemon
1 tsp dried thyme
Black pepper
Salt

Put the belly pork in the food processor and blend until quite coarse in texture. Chop the pig's liver in the same way, leaving it slightly coarse as well.

Place in a large glass mixing bowl and add the remaining ingredients, mix thoroughly and then pack into a 1 litre/2 pint terrine dish. Push in well to avoid air pockets. Cover with the lid or tightly with tin foil. Place in a *bain marie* and bake in the oven at 160°C/325°F gas mark 3 for 1–1$^1/_2$ hours.

The pâté is ready when it begins to come away from the sides. Remove from the oven. Cut a piece of cardboard the size of the pate, wrap it in foil and then place on the top and lightly weight to press the pâté. Leave for 2 hours and then place in the fridge. To remove the pâté, just immerse the mould in boiling water for 1 minute and then turn out.

poultry & game

The Great Chicken Hunt

OK, I've had great beef, lamb, fine lobster, top raspberries, sparkling bass and beetroot straight from the ground into my bag. Ask about chicken, though, and you mostly get blank looks, they probably think I am mad to ask such a daft question. Not much decent chicken round here, they say. Sure, some people might keep a few for themselves, but as for buying one, well, good luck, I'm told.

Over the last 30 or so years chicken as become a regular feature in most people's shopping baskets, a favourite with supermarkets and manufacturers alike. The next time you venture into your local supermarket, have a look at the percentage of ready meals that have chicken in them – you will be staggered. The reason for this is straight economics... they are really cheap. The average chicken in your supermarket grows really quickly, takes up very little room when being reared, their size is easy to control and labour is minimal for a whole chicken. All this process takes about 35 days – 35 days! For the manufacturer this also rings true, their hands are tied by the supermarkets pushing for ever higher margins, so they use as much chicken as possible. Another reason it is so popular is because, for manufacturer and supermarkets, chicken will carry almost any flavour, because chicken has little flavour itself. How can it with such a quick process from start to finish?

Fifty years ago, chicken was a luxury food item, and would only be enjoyed by average families on special occasions, such was the expense of buying a bird. In those days, chickens were all reared in a traditional way, with slow maturing traditional breeds, which allowed them to form correctly and develop correct bone and muscle structure. They were allowed to roam free and fed on a natural diet. Chicken was almost gamey, a treat for the cook and a real pleasure to eat. Look what it has become, a tasteless bird, with a high water content, no meaty structure to the texture, pumped full of antibiotics... indeed, it has changed beyond all recognition. People have forgotten or have never known the true taste of a real chicken.

Ok, that's the bad news. The good news is that there are many people in this country who have been rearing chickens in the traditional way for many years, and people are slowly discovering the joy of carving a chicken on a Sunday that delivers them great flavour and which is a pleasure to eat. Of course, there is a price to pay for this, although to me it is merely rebalancing the scales that have tipped too far in favour of cheap, cheap, cheap.

So, what of my dilemma? Where will I find decent chicken in these parts? Fortunately help is on hand, although communicating with this person might prove difficult. Anne Parry at Gallt y Beren Farm in Rhyd-Y-Clafdy comes to my rescue, and says she knows someone who might be able to help. In fact, I had just missed him. She was expecting him back in the afternoon, though, and would get him to call me. All very cloak-and-dagger, I thought, but that's part of the fun and anticipation of things to come. Can't I ring him I say? No, Anne says, he's not on the phone. Not on the phone! Are you kidding me, even I've got a mobile now!

Later, while relaxing at the cottage, I receive the call I have been waiting for. He introduces himself as Elwyn, and tells me he lives not far from Anne in Rhyd-Y-Clafdy, and in fact he his with her now. Not wanting to waste time, I ask about chicken. He tells me I'm a little too early, as they won't be ready for another month... disaster! Then a slight reprieve, as he tells me that if I don't mind a bird that's a little younger, then he will gladly supply me with one. How young, I ask? Ninety days, comes the reply. Hell, that's not that young! As well as this he has duck, geese and turkey. I decide I'll take a chicken and a duck. He tells me the address and to come and see him in two days to collect them, then hangs up. End of story, game on, right result!

I'm so pleased I forget to ask how much they would cost. Still I'm sure they will be worth it.

Two days later I jump in the car to travel the 20 miles to Elwyn's place, directions written on a scrap of paper on the passenger seat and looking forward to getting a decent chicken.

Quite near a pub, he told me... must be that turning there then. As I pull into the driveway it seems the last place that you would find a chicken for sale. Unperturbed I knock on the door... I'm sure he said 2pm? No-one there it seems. I knock on the neighbour's door to enquire about Elwyn's whereabouts. Gone out, I'm told, but will be back later. Strange. They ask me to leave a message and they will pass it on. Come to collect my chicken and duck. At this point the neighbour starts laughing... personally I've said funnier things in my time, but eh, if he finds it funny let him laugh. Then it becomes apparent that I am in the wrong place, and this is the wrong Elwyn. Lost again! Luckily he knows where the other Elwyn lives, and points me in the right direction. Let's hope there's only one more Elwyn in the village, or I'll be in trouble!

I study the directions again and decide to travel up the main road for a while and see what I can find. Nothing appears for about half a mile, then I come across a house set back, just off the bend of the road. Can't hurt to have a look, you never know. As I jump out of the car I am greeted by several dogs, not a good start, not great with dogs. A man comes wandering out and politely asks me who I'm looking for. Elwyn, I say; to my complete surprise he says he is Elwyn, and that I must be Ian. Bingo!!

Did I have any problems finding it, he says? Piece of cake, I say. Well, don't want him thinking I get lost for a living.

He has prepared my chicken and duck, but asks if I would like to have a look around. Walking past the house towards the area where he keeps his poultry, we walk past a pack of hounds barking loudly. His brother is into the hunting game, it seems, rather topical at the moment considering they are about to ban it.

The area where is birds are kept is just like a scene from the

Darling Buds of May, scattered everywhere, all the way down to the pond at the end of their roaming space. They are all fed on a natural diet, free to roam and have plenty of fresh water.

He mainly sells them locally to people who know him, although at Christmas demand is high for turkeys and geese, so this is a busy period. He doesn't really have a true market place for his birds because they are too expensive to sell in these parts, so it is more of a hobby than a viable business.

He even keeps some rare breed chickens, one of which, Lavender, I have never heard of. It is quite a scrawny looking bird, that yields little meat but has a fantastic flavour. He promises to let me buy one when they are ready.

As an added bonus I get to pick some bulace form his trees around the pond, and then he asks if I would like to go and look for some mushrooms. This proves fruitless, a little disappointing, but I do pick some crab apples from a tree in the centre of the farm.

Time to collect my chickens, so we pop into the house and have a cup of tea with his mum. She's been here for years and has seen many good and bad times for the farming industry. This is a bad period. All anyone wants is cheap food, she says, and no-one knows how to cook anymore.

Well it was quite a mission, but I'm finally presented with my chicken and duck and pay him £20.00 – £12.00 for the chicken and £8.00 for a fine looking Aylesbury duck.

Oh, and he also gives me a scrap of paper, with his phone number on it! I feel quite honoured.

Garlic & Lemon Roasted Chicken

Serves 4

Good quality chicken needs more care when cooking. I find cooking it a little slower and basting frequently gives great results. I used the chicken from Elwyn's in Rhyd-Y-Clafdy. This is a nice gentle way to roast a chicken, with thin slices of lemon under the skin and packed with butter. Cooking garlic for a long time will make it less harsh, and adds a great depth to the flavour of the bird. The lemon will create a great glaze to finish.

1 x 1.5kg/3lb 12oz whole chicken
1 lemon sliced
2 large sprigs rosemary
$^1/_2$ head garlic
$^1/_2$ tsp crushed chilli flakes
50g/2oz unsalted welsh butter
$^1/_2$ tsp Anglesey sea salt

Stuff the cavity of the chicken with the lemon (reserving 2 slices), garlic and rosemary. Lift up the skin on the breast and stuff in the butter and the 2 remaining slices of lemon.

Sprinkle with the flaked chillies and sea salt.

Bake at 190ºC/375ºF, gas mark 5 for 2 hours basting every 30 minutes.

Allow to rest for 20 minutes before carving.

Don't throw the carcass away, it makes great stock for soup.

Chicken Stock

1 chicken carcass, chopped
Small piece of celery
$^1/_2$ onion, peeled
$^1/_2$ leek, washed
4 clove garlic
4 black peppercorns
Few parsley stalks, sprig of rosemary, thyme and a small bay leaf

Place the carcass in a suitable pan and cover with cold water.

Bring to the boil and skim off any scum that rises to the surface. Reduce the heat and add the remaining ingredients.

Simmer very gently for about 2–3 hours.

Strain through a fine sieve and use as required.

Duck, Apple & Prunes

Serves 4–5

When I left Elwyn's in Rhyd-Y-Clafdy I was holding a large chicken and a fantastic dry plucked, free range, corn fed Aylesbury duck. When I returned to Aberdaron, I set to work creating this dish. I had some apple juice in the fridge from Hootons's and some prunes in the cupboard, a fantastic combination – the apple juice was a mixture of Discovery and Bramley, which works well, although you could use any other varieties.

For this dish I cut the legs off and cut them into the thigh and drumstick. Then placing the duck breast side up, I ran my knife straight down the centre and through the backbone. I chopped away the excess bones and put them to roast so I could make stock. Leaving the breast on the bone, I then chopped each one into 3 pieces.

You could also use whole duck legs or even whole duck for this, just extend the cooking time for the whole bird. It is cooked in the oven uncovered, which will give you crispy skin, with moist, succulent meat.

A 2kg/5lb dry plucked, free range duck, cut into 10 pieces (as explained above)
A little oil
2 medium – large onions, cut in half, then into thick wedges
4 large cloves garlic, finely sliced
16 prunes
4 good sprigs thyme
300 ml/12fl oz apple juice
Sea salt
Freshly ground black pepper

Heat the oven to 190°C/375°F gas mark 5.

Heat a large ovenproof pan or large hob/ovenproof casserole pot. Brush the base with a thin layer of vegetable oil. Season the duck with salt, then place in the hot pan and fry the pieces until well browned on the skin side. Remove from the pan and place on a plate to one side.

Reduce the heat and then add the onions and cook gently for about 10 minutes, until slightly softened.

Add the garlic, prunes and thyme. Place the duck pieces skin side up on top of the onions.

Pour in the apple juice, add a little more salt and season with black pepper.

Bring to the boil, and then place in the oven, uncovered for about an hour and 10 minutes.

I basted mine once after half an hour.

Remove from the oven and take out the duck onto a plate. Place the liquor back on the stove and bring to the boil. Reduce by about half and serve the juice with the duck.

I served this with mashed potato and some steamed pointed cabbage.

Chicken Livers on Toast, Parsley & Capers

Serves 4

I love chicken livers – they are simple to cook, very cheap and very tasty. They are best served pink, so quick cooking is essential. The best way to toast your bread is to sprinkle with olive oil and grill it in a ribbed skillet pan.

4 rashers dry cured streaky bacon
250g/9oz chicken livers, trimmed
55g/2oz finely chopped shallot
80g/3oz butter
2 tbsps capers
1 tbsp roughly chopped flat leaf parsley
Salt and black pepper
4 slices of thick bread, toasted in a skillet pan
25g/1oz mixed leaves, mizuna, rocket and red mustard leaves.
A little red wine and shallot dressing (see p. 71)

Start by grilling the bacon until it is crispy.

Heat a frying pan and add 25g butter, before the butter starts to brown add the chicken livers and shallots, season with salt and black pepper. Cook over a medium-high heat for about 1/1$\frac{1}{2}$ minutes on each side, if they are large allow a little longer.

Remove the chicken livers from the pan and keep on a plate. Add the remaining butter to the pan and increase the heat. When the butter is a nutty brown, add the capers, parsley and the chicken livers.

Place salad leaves on the toast, top with chicken livers and drizzle with a little red wine and shallot dressing.

Guinea Fowl, Leeks & Mustard

Serves 4

The breasts I used for this recipe came from Hooton's in Anglesey. They were quite large, so the cooking time may well vary if yours are a lot smaller. This is a simple dish that is all cooked in one pan, just make sure you cook the leeks enough... nothing worse than crunchy leeks.

2 breasts guinea fowl
Knob of butter
Splash of vegetable oil
1 small leek, washed and finely sliced
1 shallot, finely sliced
1 rasher of dry cured bacon
1 clove garlic, crushed
50ml/2 fl oz white wine
100ml/4fl oz double cream
1 generous tsp whole grain mustard
Salt and black pepper

Heat a frying pan or sauté pan that preferably has a lid. Add the butter and oil. Season the guinea fowl, place in the pan and brown on both sides. Remove from the pan and keep to one side.

Reduce the heat and add the leeks, shallot and bacon. Coat with the fat, cover with a lid and gently cook for about 5 minutes. Add the garlic and the wine. Place the guinea fowl in the pan skin side up. Add a couple of tablespoons of water and cover with the lid. Cook over a gentle heat for about 10–15 minutes.

Remove the lid and add the cream, mustard and a little seasoning. Bring to the boil and simmer until the right consistency is achieved.

Guinea Fowl & Leek Pie

Serves 6

This can be made exactly the same way with chicken.

1.5–1.7 kg/3lb-3lb 8oz guinea fowl
1 large onion, chopped
2 small leeks, sliced
2 cloves garlic, crushed
25g/1oz flour
25g/1oz butter
500ml/20fl oz cooking liquor
300ml/12fl oz double cream
Salt and black pepper

1 recipe short crust pastry or puff pastry (see p. 147)

Remove the legs and breast from the guinea fowl. Chop up the carcass. Put the chopped carcass, legs and breast in a suitable pan. Pour enough cold water over to cover. Place on the heat and bring to the boil. Remove any scum that rises to the top. Reduce the heat and simmer gently for about 1 hour.

Remove the meat from the liquor and place on a plate to cool. Strain the liquid through a fine sieve. Discard the carcass. Measure out 500ml/1 pint and keep hot.

In a saucepan, melt the butter, add the onion and sweat until soft Add the flour. Cook over a low heat for about 3 minutes, stirring a couple of times. Gradually add the hot liquid and stir in, ensuring no lumps. When the sauce is smooth, add the leeks, garlic and seasoning. Simmer gently for about 5 minutes. Add the double cream, stir in well and remove from the heat.

Remove the skin from the guinea fowl pieces and then take all the meat from the legs. Chop the breast meat into large pieces.

Place the meat in suitable pie dish. Pour over the sauce with the leeks. Leave to cool down for 30 minutes.

Roll out the pastry and use to cover the dish. Using a small sharp knife, pierce the top of the pastry. Brush will a little beaten whole egg and place in an oven 220°C/425°F, gas mark 7 for about 10 minutes to set the pastry and then reduce the heat to 200°C/400°F, gas mark 6 and cook for a further 45 minutes.

Pot Roasted Rabbit, Lemon & Rosemary

Serves 2–3

I don't eat rabbit often, but I remember a dish we used to cook at Bank restaurant in London. We took the legs which were boned out and then stuffed with lots of butter, herbs and lemon. They were then individually wrapped in foil and roasted for about 12 minutes. The result was extremely moist meat with that great hint of lemon.

For this dish I have jointed a whole rabbit, which depending on the size will give you 6–8 pieces. When I cooked this my rabbit was quite small, so I only had six pieces; two legs, two shoulders and the saddle cut into two across the bone. The rabbit is then sautéed in a generous amount of butter, and gently cooked with a little wine.

1 wild rabbit, jointed (as explained above)
Salt and pepper
75g/3oz butter
Splash of olive oil
3 wide strips lemon peel
2 sprigs rosemary
4 cloves garlic, sliced
100ml/4fl oz dry white wine

Heat a heavy, thick bottomed pan and heat the butter with a splash of olive oil. Season the rabbit pieces and then brown over a medium heat on both sides. This should take about 5 minutes. Remove the saddle pieces and leave on a plate.

Add the lemon peel, rosemary, garlic and coat with the butter and cook for 1–2 minutes.

Add the white wine, bring to the boil and then reduce the heat.
Cover with a lid and cook very gently for 20 minutes.

Add the pieces of saddle back to the pan and cover with the lid,
continue to cook for 15 minutes.

Remove the rabbit from the pan and reduce the liquid a little.
Serve with the rabbit.

Game Stock

If you eat game, you will always have left over bones, either from cooked carcass or after preparing forcemeats for terrines, etc. They make a delicious stock that you can use for making gravy, sauces and for flavouring soups, as in the pheasant and cabbage soup.

1.4kg/3lb game bones, roasted
Water
6 peppercorns
6 juniper berries
Selection of herbs
4 cloves garlic
Few scraps of leek
1 small onion, cut in half
Small stick celery, roughly chopped
1 small carrot, roughly chopped
1 dessert spoon of tomato paste

Place all the ingredients in a suitable pan.

Pour enough cold water over to cover.

Place on the stove and then bring to the boil. Remove any scum that rises to the top.

Reduce the heat and simmer very gently for about $2^1/_2$ hours. Strain through a fine sieve and use as required.

Pot Roasted Pheasant & Beetroot

Serves 2

There are two stages to cooking the pheasant in this dish. The legs need a long cook, as they can be quite tough otherwise. You add the breast towards the end to maintain its moisture.

This is a great way to cook, though, where everything goes in one pan and helps develop many different flavours that will enhance your sauce at the end.

1 pheasant, legs and breasts removed
200g/8oz peeled wedges of beetroot
200g/8oz peeled wedges of onion (red or white)

Using a wide-based, ovenproof pan or baking dish, chop the carcass in two and place in the bottom. Place the pheasant legs on top and then scatter round the beetroot and onions. Add a generous knob of butter and season everything with sea salt and black pepper.

Add some sprigs of thyme and then place in the oven at 230ºC/450ºF, gas mark 8 for 10 minutes. When the pheasant has started to brown, reduce the heat to gas mark 6 and cover with a lid or tin foil.

Cook for about 30 minutes. Remove the lid and place in the breasts. Cook for about 10–15 minutes.

Pheasant, Apples & Shallots

Serves 2

The idea for this recipe came about because I had taken the legs off and put them to confit with some other pheasants. Left with just the crown, I decided upon the idea of pot roasting.

Generally, game benefits from being cooked on the bone, which retains moisture, due to the little fat that it naturally contains. So I spatchcocked it to flatten it out and trimmed a little of the back bone away. In Normandy they cook a similar dish with apples, calvados and cream. I've not used cream, but you can add a little at the end if you wish.

1 crown pheasant
Splash of vegetable oil
Good knob of butter
2 shallots, peeled and sliced
2 small apples, I used Fiesta here, peeled, cored and each one
  cut into 8
Capful of brandy
200ml/8fl oz game stock
Salt and black pepper

Start by turning the bird onto its breast. Take a large knife and split down the back bone – alternatively, a strong pair of heavy-duty scissors might do the trick. Push firmly down with the palm of your hand and flatten the bird out. Trim off the excess back bone – this can be saved for stock. Season with salt and black pepper.

Heat a thick bottom sauté pan and add the oil and butter. When it begins to froth, add the pheasant skin side down and brown it quickly. Turn the bird over and then reduce the heat. Cover with a lid and then cook gently for about 25 minutes, basting occasionally.

Remove the pheasant and place on a plate to one side.

Add the shallots and cook gently for 2 minutes, then add the apples, and toss into the butter. Cook for about 3–4 minutes, so they just begin to soften.

Increase the heat and add the brandy; after a minute add the stock and any other juices from the pheasant.

Reduce the liquor by roughly half.

Split the pheasant down the middle and serve with the sauce.

.

Pheasant Broth

Serves 8-10

A good way to use up slightly older game birds towards the end of the season. Keeping the pheasant on the bone flavours the stock naturally without addition of other stock. You can either keep the pieces whole when you eat the soup, or remove them and strip the meat off and put the torn pieces of meat back in.

1 pheasant
2 litres/ about 4 pints water
1 bouquet garni
3 juniper berries, split in half
200g/8oz pointed cabbage, washed and chopped
1 medium onion, coarsely chopped
2 cloves garlic, sliced thinly
200g/8ozcarrots, peeled and chopped
400g/1lb potato, peeled and diced
Salt and Black pepper

Chop up the pheasant into 8 pieces and place in a suitable saucepan. Cover with the water and add the bouquet garni, juniper berries and onions. Bring to the boil and skim any scum off that rises to the surface. When you have done this reduce the heat and simmer gently for 1 hour.

Add the garlic, carrots, potato and season well with salt and pepper. Simmer gently until the vegetables are just cooked, add the cabbage and stri well.

Simmer for about 5 minutes until the cabbage is cooked but still has a slight bite.

Roast Wild Duck, Tayberry & Orange Sauce

Serves 2

Wild duck is a very different proposition than a normal duck like Aylesbury or Gressingham. It has little or no fat, so needs a quick roast and to be served pink, or it will be dry.

Tayberries are a cross between a raspberry and blackberry, aromatic and perfumed. I bought a pot of jam made from them at Hooton's, and decided to add a spoonful to the sauce for this recipe. It works very well and adds a nice fruity touch to the dish.

1 wild duck
Tayberry jam
100ml/4fl oz red wine
2 tsps red wine vinegar
200ml/8fl oz game stock
Finely grated orange zest

Season the duck, inside and out. Heat a small roasting tray or thick bottom pan suitable for the oven. Add a splash of vegetable oil and a knob of butter. Add the duck breast side down and brown quickly for 2 minutes. Turn it over and then place in the oven at 200ºC/400ºF, gas mark 6. It will need cooking for about 30 minutes, and you should baste it twice during cooking. Remove the duck from the pan and leave on a plate. Drain most of the oil and place back on a hot stove. Add 100ml/4fl oz red wine and 2 tsps red wine vinegar. Boil to reduce by half. Add 200ml/8fl oz game stock, a heaped teaspoon of tayberry jam and a little finely grated orange zest. Bring to the boil and reduce by about half. Add any juices from the duck. Pass the sauce through a fine sieve.

Carve the duck and serve with the sauce.

vegetables

Two Jobs – One Passion

Jill works three days a week, nothing strange in that. Mike works five days a week, looks like he needs to be looking at the marriage contract! Ok, so nothing strange in that either. Well, here is the strange thing... they also find time to run an organic fruit and vegetable farm. Are they mad, how is this possible? So why the dedication, why inconvenience yourself, why do something that is so financially unrewarding?

It wasn't supposed to be like this, explained Jill. The original plan was to be self-sufficient, grow enough for themselves, keep a bit of livestock and live happily in the beautiful rural, idyllic countryside of LLangybi. Well, it certainly is a stunning setting, with views of distant mountains and miles and miles of lush fields. It also happens to be another stunning day – seems I'm getting off lightly; well I think perhaps I should roll with it and enjoy it while it lasts.

Thursday is picking day, so it's all hands to the pump. That is Jill, myself and the wise and affable Andy, a retired Cornishman who has time on his hands and loves getting his hands dirty.

Jill farms organically, which in itself presents many challenges. She converted four years ago, and has Soil Association accreditation – that is expensive enough, and when you consider the premium they pay for organic products (seed and feed can cost up to twice as much as non-organic), the economics seemed to be stacked against them. Indeed, each year she and her husband ask 'will this be their last year?' It seems Mike believes they deserve more of a life, can you blame him? This is a seven day operation, heavily dependent on the weather.

Picking is extremely time consuming, so any extra help is gratefully received by Jill. Could she afford to pay for help? No, instead she relies on the 'you give me a hand and I'll send you off with some veggies' routine. Sounds great to me, and anyway food is as good as money and at least I know where it has come from.

Today we are bean bashing, well runner beans and dwarf beans, the French beans have just come to the end. Jill has already done the potatoes for this week, so that is one less job. She's teamed up with her neighbour Val... sounds familiar, that name... ah yes, she would be the one I asked directions from – not that I was lost or anything! Together they supply about 40 vegetable boxes to their loyal customers every Friday. Indeed they have a list of people waiting in the wings. Being seasonal you are never guaranteed what you will get, so how do her customers find this? When they first started the scheme, she confesses people looked a bit bemused – after all, everyone is so used to year-round supply that it does come as a bit of a shock when you can't get what you want. Over time, though, they have got used to it, and quite enjoy the surprise. They do try their best to give variety, and this is where they make the difference. They can experiment a bit more, be more flexible and grow things with more flavour. They can also guarantee that all the vegetables are picked on the day of delivery, or at least the day before, and their customers know exactly where the produce comes from – the benefits stay in the local community.

So is it a success? Well, that would depend on how you judge the term 'success'. Commercially it seems like complete and utter madness, but that would be to miss the point. Spiritually it seems like a lifeline, keeping the connection with the land, supporting the local community and giving people top quality produce. In an industry that is rapidly being condensed by the large retailers, who are only interested in large profits and not necessarily good quality, then their enterprise is a roaring success.

We don't discuss supermarkets too much, but Jill does announce her disappointment with the quality and value for money of the supermarkets' organic produce, and that a large percentage of it isn't grown in the British Isles. This, she says, is not a true representation of the quality of organic food.

All the supermarkets want is varieties that will keep for longer; shelf life is the driver, not taste. Does the public know any different? Certain age groups may, but it is the younger generation who need the education, and this is sadly lacking. It's sad to think that in the future people might think that all lettuces grow with seven coloured leaves, come in a plastic pack and sells for £1.29. They may also think that there are only four or five different varieties of apple in the world. Jill actually has 40, yes *40,* varieties, a serious commitment to growing for flavour, and her contribution is much needed to support one of Britain's greatest fruits. We have some of the finest tasting apples in the world, a fact not disputed by experts, so where, may I ask, are they?!

Beans picked, we head off for the greenhouse to pick some tomatoes, aubergines and basil. On the way past the house, Jill shows me the shitake mushrooms she has been growing, popping out of bits of old wood lined up against the window sill. They smell incredible, and she takes one and offers us a piece. Nicer cooked, I'm thinking, but then it is rude not to accept things that are given to you. The flavour is smoky, nutty and very intense.

Her greenhouse is not particularly large, but the smells are inviting. We pick some great tasting cherry tomatoes, bursting with sweetness and flavour, perfect for sauces I think. She gathers up some basil, picks a few aubergines and then notices the time... whoops, seems we should be leaving. We head off to the house and have a quick drink, chew the fat a little more and then Andy and I go and get the trailer that we have already loaded with most things. We just need to grab the potatoes and we can be off. We position the trailer onto the back off the car, still complete with two kayaks that Jill is looking forward to getting in the water later, if she gets time.

On arrival at Val's we get stuck straight in. Well, to lunch anyway. Val's husband and Londoner Eddy join us; they are busy building a cottage to let to tourists in the holiday season. This is a regular theme in the area, and helps to supplement the farming.

Val has a fairly substantial polytunnel, in which she grows various varieties of tomato, four types of cucumber, aubergines, strawberries and sweetcorn. Outside she has a glut of raspberries which are ripe for picking. Andy waxes lyrical about the magic of raspberries, 'the king of soft fruit' he announces. Hard to disagree.

So, on with the packing, Val and Jill have a quick board meeting about who's got what, how much will each box get, have we got enough and what the split of large and small boxes will be. Behind us there is a little whiteboard hanging... this will be where the list is compiled.

Andy, who decided to skip lunch, has already packed the cherry tomatoes into punnets and topped each one with a small bunch of basil, added value indeed, we all laugh! Me, I'm given potato duty... today's variety is 'verity', a white potato with a very dry matter, apparently preferred by their customers. One pound, twelve ounces for the small boxes and two pounds, eight ounces for the large... what no kilos?!

Usually they pack on their own, so maybe they think they'll finish quicker with Andy and I helping. Jill asks me whether she should mix the different kinds of beans together. I say no, but she mixes them anyway. There's some great looking stuff here, different types of chard, courgettes, garlic, shallots and a cucumber the size of a marrow, and I'm not kidding either. Do you think this would go into Tesco, Jill jokes?

Andy and I fix together the boxes and the packing begins. A stroll round the table with a bag of this and bag of that, making sure heavy stuff is in the bottom. Brian and Eddy pop in from time to time to saw and drill and generally make as much noise as possible. Seems we don't have enough tomatoes, so Val rushes off to pick some more and I join her. That done we load all the boxes into the trailer and begin the journey to the shop, although while gently positioning the trailer to leave, we crash into some of Eddy's handiwork... hmm, not sure they should be that bent.

Most of their customers pay in advance by cheque, but they still also operate an honesty policy box too. Everyone is very good at this, and Val says her major problem is preventing people taking her prized jams and chutneys she has lined up like soldiers. Raspberry seems to be particular favourite... hands off, Andy!

Time for a well earned cuppa and a slice of chocolate cake. The cake brings immediate controversy to the table and here's why. The cake is from the Co-op, and is under their fair-trade logo. Jill has flipped onto the ingredients and discovers that battery farmed eggs have been used: Brian doesn't believe this, and asks for a closer look. Astonished, he informs her that he will write a letter to them, which she also agrees to do. This just leaves the question of whether they going to eat any – obviously this is a tricky one, and they will have to battle with their consciences. They eventually succumb to temptation!

They are expecting a change in the weather tomorrow, rain is coming and so Andy volunteers to pick the raspberries. Not wishing to let him have all the fun, I'm on my toes to join him.

It's a painstakingly slow process. They seem to be hiding everywhere, and no matter how hard you look there are bound to be a few that slip your beady eye. It also doesn't help that we are stuffing our faces with many that we pick. A couple of hours of picking, chatting, eating, singing and then I look towards what we have picked, and I can't believe it – is that it? Who stole the rest? I've picked for all that time, I look like a mass bloody murderer and that's it! Where's the justice in that?

It's about 7pm now; it's been a long but highly satisfying day, time to collect my reward. I'm presented with a bag of veggies, which includes one of Jill's prized aubergines and some punnets of delicious, fragrant raspberries. Seasonally happy, I say my goodbyes and head for the gate, just beating Andy to it.

I hope that things continue to go well for Jill, Mike and Val, and they keep supplying great local produce to people who care about where their food comes from.

Anyone for kayaking?!

Baked Aubergines, Courgette & Tomato

Serves 4

At the end of a hard day's picking and packing with Jill and Val I'm rewarded with a bag of goodies, including, I'm told luckily, one of Jill's prized aubergines. Let's cook it before she asks for it back then!

The thing with aubergines is that, in my opinion they benefit from long cooking to bring out the best in them. The great aubergine dishes of the world like Imam Bayaldi, smoky aubergine purees from the middle east and north Africa, and even in the good old moussaka, they are all very soft. It brings out the creamy nature of the vegetable.

For this particular dish I wouldn't salt the aubergines. The length of cooking will take any bitterness away. And remember, there is nothing worse than undercooked aubergine... cook and cook! Also, this dish relies upon the flavour from good tomatoes, so smell them first – no smell, no good.

Slice one large aubergine lengthways about 5mm thick. Do the same with three courgettes. Slice a large beefsteak tomato or a similar quantity of tomatoes of your choice.

Place the aubergine in a suitable ovenproof dish, top with a layer of courgette and then all the tomato, and season with salt and black pepper. Scatter over a few whole leaves of basil and two crushed cloves of garlic. Layer the remaining courgettes, then finish with the aubergines. Drizzle with 4 tbsps olive oil.

Cover with foil and bake for about 40 minutes at 200ºC/400ºF, gas mark 6.

Remove the foil and cook for another 10 minutes to colour the top.

Tagliatelle, Crushed Tomatoes & Courgettes

Serves 4

We picked these tomatoes in the morning at Jill and Mike's. I was totally intoxicated by the smell of the little red fruits. Their natural sweetness, deep red colour and intense flavour were a joy. Absolutely perfect for this dish, which lives and dies by the flavour of the tomatoes. It is really fresh tasting because you don't cook the tomatoes for very long.

2 tbsps olive oil
500g/1lb 4oz cherry tomatoes
1 recipe of fresh tagliatelle (see p. 33), or top quality bought one
2 cloves crushed garlic
1 medium courgette

For the sauce put 2 tbsps olive oil in a wide surface pan. Add 500g/1lb 4oz cherry tomatoes, which you can crush in your hands over the pan, so you don't lose any juice.

Cook over a high heat for 5–6 minutes. Add 2 cloves crushed garlic and 1 medium courgette cut into ribbons, about the thickness of the tagliatelle. Season with a little sea salt and grind in some black pepper. Simmer gently for 5 minutes.

Cook the tagliatelle in plenty of rapidly boiling salted water for about 2–3 minutes. Drain and add to the sauce. Toss it all together and serve with plenty of freshly grated hard, sharp goats cheese.

Beetroot & Blue Cheese Salad

Serves 4

200g/8oz diced cooked beetroot
1 red onion, chopped
75g/3oz Gorau Glas cheese
50g/2oz mixed leaves
8 walnut halves, broken up into pieces
2 tbsps balsamic dressing
Salt and pepper

Whisk up 100ml/4fl oz balsamic vinegar with 200ml/8fl oz olive oil and 200ml/8fl oz groundnut oil. Add some salt and pepper. Store in a bottle and use as required.

Toss all the ingredients in a bowl and serve.

Beetroot, Carrot & Orange Salad

Serves 4

Try to choose young beetroot and carrots for this – it will be really juicy and makes a superior salad.

300g/12oz beetroot peeled and grated
200g/8oz carrots, peeled and grated
Zest and juice of $^1/_2$ orange
2 tbsps of red wine vinegar
Good splash of olive oil
Sea salt and black pepper

Place all the ingredients in a bowl and toss well together.

Adding roughly chopped flat leaf parsley is a great addition to this.

Foil Roasted Beetroot

Serves 4

3 medium beetroot, peeled and cut into 1"/12.5cm chunks
2 cloves garlic, peeled and cut in half
1 tsp balsamic vinegar
Good splash of olive oil
Anglsey sea salt and freshly ground black pepper

Place all the ingredients on a sheet of tin foil.

Season with the salt and pepper and wrap securely.

Bake in the oven at 180ºC/375ºF, gas mark 5 for about 1 hour.

Broad Bean & Mint Risotto

Serves 4

Fresh broad beans are really delicious, although they are a little time consuming. If you are lucky and they are very young you will not have to peel them. Risotto is one of the most satisfying dishes to cook, and if you follow a few golden rules you will never go wrong. First, you must buy the correct rice – arborio, carnaroli, vialone nano; secondly, always add the stock a little at a time. I usually do this in three stages. Thirdly, never, ever leave a risotto on its own; you must keep it company at all times. Lastly, a plea: never, ever finish with cream. I can't understand this practice, which would make an Italian lose sleep! Finally, always use a wooden spoon.

Thanks to Joyce and Emylyn up the hill in Aberdaron for supplying the broad beans and peas, a local haven of windswept pleasure.

If the broad beans are quite big you will need to blanch them in boiling water for 1 minute.

You will need 450g/1lb 2oz broad beans for this recipe.

Drain them and place them in ice cold water. Peel them and keep them to one side for later.

Heat 2 tbsps olive oil in a suitable pan and add 2 finely chopped shallots and sauté over a gentle heat for 5 minutes, until slightly softened. Add 75g/3oz risotto rice, 1 clove of crushed garlic and coat with the shallots and oil. Add 50ml/ 2fl oz dry white wine and 100ml/4fl oz hot stock(you will need about 300ml of vegetable stock in total).

Cook over a medium heat until all the stock is soaked up. Repeat this process until all of the stock is gone. This should take about 15 minutes. The rice should have a creamy coating, but have little bite.

Add 50g/2oz blanched fresh peas, shelled broad beans, 2tsp chopped mint, 2tsp chopped parsley and 50g/2oz freshly grated firm, sharp goat's cheese. Serve immediately.

Courgette, French Bean Salad with Roasted Beetroot

Serves 4

Use the foil roasted beetroot recipe for that part of this salad.

1 courgette, sliced in half lengthways and cut into 5mm half moon slices, blanched for 1 minute and refreshed
125g/5oz cooked French beans
75g/3oz roasted beetroot

For the dressing, put 1 egg yolk in a bowl, add the juice of 1 lemon and gradually whisk in 100ml/4fl oz groundnut oil and 100 ml/4fl oz olive oil. You need to do this very slowly at first to avoid it splitting. Stir in 50g/2oz finely firm, sharp goat's cheese.

Place all the salad ingredients in a bowl and add 2 tbsps of dressing or more if you like. Twist in some black pepper and toss together.

To Goat or Not to Goat?

I'd spoken to Anne Parry a few times on the phone from London, a quietly spoken lady, almost with a childlike, shy quality, so much so I had to rapidly increase the volume on the phone, just so I could comprehend what she was saying. I think it was Joyce from Aberdaron that had told me about her, and said I should get in touch, as she made delicious goats cheese.

See, that's how these things work – once you know one person, you know two, then three, four, five, six, seven... until you've built up a massive network of good food contacts and had a lot of fun tracking down phone numbers, speaking to them, getting directions, jumping in the car, speaking to lovely ladies in post offices, pub landlords and local bus drivers. Then, with any luck you might just track down the person you set out to find. In this age of high-powered technology, with websites that will do it all for you, you know the ones. Tap in your starting destination and your intended port of call and bingo, there it all is on screen. The quickest route, the time taken, roundabouts and coffee en route! Personally I find it all very dull, boring, predictable and without any sense of risk or adventure. Much better to get the directions from the source, cruise around the village a few times and have a chat with a few locals, which on occasion can be confusing, but never without a few laughs, and perhaps a few mishaps.

Anne's farm is in Rhyd-y-Clafdy, only a few miles from Pwllheli, and one of the few places I actually found first time, no mean feat for me. I'd been told she lived on an estate – good job I brushed off my best Barbour, pressed my fine slacks and polished up the wellies... you know, the ones with holes in. Well, I always get a heightened sense of grandeur when I hear the term 'estate'... lords and ladies of the manor, different species, people who don't live in my world.

Before you enter the drive there is a small plaque, telling you the name, and that this farm is certified organic by the Soil Association. A short drive up, pass what turns out to be the original house, where her mum resides, and destination front door reached. This looks quite normal... old cars lying about that look like their road days are over, a few bits of scattered machinery, several out-buildings and people working next to the house. These, as it turn out, are Anne's sons, who are fixing an urgent water problem. How bad is it I ask? Well, we don't have any, comes the short reply. Ok, that seems urgent enough. He downs tools and shouts for Anne. Now I don't know why, but I had this image of Anne in my head. A tough, well-built lady and not one to mix her words, surely not possible with such a softly spoken women. Stupid, I know, and also quickly dispelled. For, when she arrives, she's a slim, slender looking lady, almost frail. She looks cold, goose pimples all over her small arms. I swear, if I'd have blown on her she would have come a cropper and be heading for a compulsory 10 count. Don't judge a book and all that...

Never more so than in this case. A person who has passion for something will have a strong identity, a fierce dedication and not much fear of fighting others who don't share their viewpoint. Welcome to the real Anne Parry – and she's only cold because the house is perishing, it's warmer outside.

Anne's been farming for 25 years, since she married her husband, whose family have been here through many generations. They converted to organic four years ago, citing the huge potential in that market. Their main source of income here is from their herd of dairy cows, among them some Jerseys. Turning organic was initially very successful indeed, and like many in the area, they joined the co-operative that is the South Caenarfon Creamy, where they send milk to be processed. Much of the milk is then distributed throughout Wales and the UK. She has good things to say about the way it is run, and says the relationship is healthy. What isn't so healthy is the price she gets paid for her milk.

We are now where she keeps some of her goats, and she hugs

one as she tells me how bad it is. The price is plummeting, she says. When she first converted to organic she could command 27 pence a litre for cows' milk. Now, she says the figure is around 21 pence a litre, and heading in one direction only. That's a significant drop, a 25% price reduction, although you probably haven't seen this reduction passed on in your supermarket. Although the price is very low, she has to feed, water and maintain the animals, so some money is obviously better than nothing.

So where do the goats come in? This was Anne's son's idea. He was studying at the local agriculture college and his thesis was written on goats, and the potentially huge market for products from them. He discussed it with his mother, and although initially reluctant, he managed to convince her to go for it and explore the options. This she did and, with a bit of research, she heard of a lady that kept goats in the area and who also produced cheese from the milk. She also happened to be retiring, and so Anne came along at just the right time. She bought all the goats, and was also kindly presented with the cheese recipes and offered any help she needed to set it up. This advice she gratefully took, for she knew nothing of cheese making. Indeed, she is sometimes helped by the lady in a more practical way when she needs it.

She also had to learn to look after goats, apparently very different to caring for sheep and cattle. She tells me they need a lot more love and personal attention, so are more time-consuming. They all have very different personalities, so the method of farming is closely built to the relationship she builds with them. She seems to enjoy it, and it offers a little more variety than her normal routine. At the moment her audience is limited, due to certain regulations imposed by the local environmental health authority. She is unable to sell her cheese to retailers, like the two delicatessens in Pwllheli. This is a real shame, not only for her but also for the shops who would otherwise definitely offer her cheeses to their customers. Instead, she relies on direct sales from her farm, some food festivals that happen in the area, and she also attends some farmers' markets.

The markets have been good for her, although Bangor could do with more stalls to attract more customers. She is slowly building a loyal following with her customers, who are delighted at the opportunity to buy some original, local cheeses. They love to buy local specialties, though Anne says they demand top quality, which is what she strives for. She still has to explain to people that the character of cheeses can change during the year, when the milk may be a little different. Although she mostly produces goats' cheese, she also makes a few cows' cheeses, and she lets me sample one. Made like a cheddar, it was really creamy. She tells me that the milk used to make it contained a good percentage of milk from her Jersey cows, but next week she may make it with no Jersey milk. Slowly, people are beginning to see this as a unique strength, and not a lack of consistency.

She produces many goats' cheeses, all of which are based on the classic popular cheeses from Britain – Wensleydale, Stilton, Cheshire, Double Gloucester and Caerphilly are a few examples. She also makes a few much softer cheeses that are lighter and more creamy in texture. They are very pronounced in their flavours, and many of them are well suited to cooking with. Indeed, you'ill find many recipes throughout the book where they are included. The sharp flavour of the Caerphilly, with its unique goat quality, complements the humble leeks and red onions in the tart on page 147. And again, it used to great effect in the Welsh Rabbit recipe on page 217.

Anne, has strong views on many issues, and is passionate about local produce and food, supporting the local economy. She also used to grow and sell potatoes, only recently giving it up. She hopes to see a move away from intensive farming, better animal welfare, more localised foods and, above all, she seeks respect.

She remains philosophical about the future, and is determined to make it work. Like her goats, she has a very distinct personality, and in harmony with them she hopes to keep progressing. How far can she go, that is the question?

Leek, Red Onion & Caerphilly Goats Cheese Tart

Serves 8

I got this delicious goats cheese version of Caerphilly from Anne Parry's farm. It is quite a sharp cheese which is the perfect foil for the sweet onions and leeks.

Short crust pastry
200g/8oz plain flour
100g/4oz hard butter, chopped
salt

300g/12oz finely sliced red onions
1 leek, sliced
3 medium eggs
100ml/4fl oz milk
200ml/8fl oz double cream
200g/4oz Caerphilly cheese
25g/1oz butter

Rub the butter into the flour and pinch of salt until it resembles breadcrumbs. Make a large well and add some water, a little at a time, bring it all together to form a dough. Do not knead this dough or it will produce slightly tough pastry. Place in greaseproof paper and put in the fridge for 20 minutes.

Roll out the pastry and use to line an 8"/20cm, loose bottomed flan case. Bake blind in an oven at 220ºC/425ºF, gas mark 7 for about 10 minutes.

Meanwhile, gently sauté the finely sliced red onions, and the sliced leeks in the butter. Cover with a lid and cook for about 20 minutes. Season well with salt and pepper.

Add the mix to the baked pastry case.

Whisk up the eggs with the milk, double cream and a little salt and black pepper. Pour over the onion mix. Sprinkle with the Caerphilly cheese.

Bake for about 35 minutes at 200ºC/400ºF, gas mark 6 or until set and lightly brown.

Onion & Blue Cheese Tart

Serves 8

This tart relies on the sweetness of the onions and the power of the blue cheese. You must make sure the onions are really soft and all the liquid has evaporated before removing them from the heat. Blue cheese can be really strong, so a light hand with the salt is recommended.

800g/2lb sliced white onions
25g/1oz butter
Salt and black pepper
75g/3oz blue cheese

Pastry
200g/8oz plain flour
50g/2oz butter
50g/2oz lard
Pinch of salt
Water to mix

Heat the butter in a large pan and add the onions. Cover with a lid and cook over a gentle heat for about 30 minutes, or until really soft. If there is a lot of liquid, simply continue to cook them over a higher heat until it has evaporated. Allow to cool.

Make the pastry by rubbing the fats into the flour and a pinch of salt until well incorporated and like breadcrumbs. Add enough water to form a smooth dough, wrap in cling film and allow to rest in the fridge for 30 minutes.

Roll out two-thirds of the pastry and use to line an 8"/20cm loose bottom flan ring or shallow cake ring.

Put the cooked onion mix in the base, spread evenly and crumble over the blue cheese.

Roll out the remaining pastry. Wet the edges of the pastry in the case and top with the rolled out pastry. Cut away any excess and gently push together the pastry. Brush with a little beaten egg.

Bake in an oven at 220°C/425°F, gas mark 7 for 10 minutes, then reduce the heat to 200°C/400°F gas mark 6 for about 30 minutes.

Remove from the oven and allow to cool.

Remove from the flan ring.

Hooton's Produce Availability

JAN: beetroot, swede, carrots, leeks, sprouting broccoli, sprouts, onions, red onions, shallots, garlic, cabbage, potatoes, parsnips, apples

FEB: as above

MARCH: as above

APRIL: potatoes, spring greens
End of April: rhubarb and asparagus

MAY: asparagus, strawberries, gooseberries, early potatoes, herbs

JUNE: asparagus (finishes 23rd) strawberries, raspberries, broad beans, french beans, peas, early beetroot, carrots, garlic (end of June), potatoes, herbs

JULY: strawberries,tayberries, raspberries, blackcurrants, redcurrants, whitecurrants, blackberries, red cabbage, calabrese, carrots, beetroot, garlic, french beans, broad beans, peas, potatoes, herbs, salad leaves, tomatoes

AUGUST: apples (Discovery), strawberries, Victoria plums, peas, broad beans, tomatoes, beetroot, carrot, french beans, potatoes, herbs, salad leaves,red cabbage, calabrese, shallots, white onions, red onions

SEPTEMBER: apples: Fiesta, Bramley, Gala, Red Falstaff, Crown Gold, Queen Cox, Howgate Wonder, Spartan, Greensleeves. Strawberries, raspberries, carrots, beetroot, white onions, red onions, garlic, tomatoes, herbs, salad leaves, calabrese, potatoes, swede, parsnips, leeks, shallots

OCTOBER: apples, strawberries, raspberries, sprouts, parsnips, carrots, leeks, sprouts, sprouting broccoli, cabbage, beetroot, shallots, white onions, red onions, herbs, salad leaves, swede

NOVEMBER: apples, sprouts, sprouting broccoli, parsnips, carrots, leeks, cabbage, beetroot, shallots, white onions, red onions, salad leaves,potatoes, swede

DECEMBER: same as above

Jill Langley's Produce Availability

JAN: beetroot, leeks, carrots, onions, rocket, lettuce, shallots, garlic, squashes, sprouts, sprouting broccoli, parsnips, curly kale, Russian red kale, pursalanne, savoy cabbage, January king cabbage, romanesco, swede, chards, pak choi, mizuna, apples, pears

FEB: same as above

MARCH: same as above

APRIL–JUNE: no boxes available to public

JULY: new potatoes, spring cabbage, broad beans, cherry tomatoes, lettuce, rocket, spring onions, courgettes, spinach, carrots, beetroot, sugar snaps, tomatoes, raspberries, strawberries, white onions, peas, cucumbers, calabrese, basil.

AUGUST: broad beans, lettuce, rocket, cherry tomatoes, spring onions, courgettes, carrots, beetroot, aubergines, peppers, summer cabbage, french beans, purple beans, runner beans, onions, peas, cucumber, basil, kohlrabi, garlic, fennel, raspberries, sugar snaps, potatoes, Emneth apples

SEPTEMBER: broad beans, cherry tomatoes, lettuce, rocket, spring onions, courgettes, spinach, carrots, beetroot, sugar snaps, tomatoes, aubergines, peppers, runner beans, french beans, purple beans, raspberries, peas, cucumber, onions, calabrese, fennel, kohlrabi, squashes, red cabbage, basil, summer cabbage, potatoes, charlotte potatoes. Keswick Codlin apples, Sunset apples, Worcester Pearmain apples, pears

OCTOBER: leeks, rocket, lettuce, cherry tomatoes, tomatoes, spring onions, courgettes, spinach, carrots, beetroot, sugar snaps, aubergines, peppers, summer cabbage, runner beans french beans, purple beans, raspberries, cucumber, onions, calabrese, kohlrabi, garlic, squashes, red cabbage, basil, potatoes, charlotte potatoes, bulb fennel, apples, pears, romanesco

NOVEMBER: leeks, cherry tomatoes, tomatoes, lettuce, rocket, spring onions, courgettes, carrots, beetroot, peppers, cucumber, kohlrabi, garlic, squashes, parsley, rosemary, thyme, sage, bay leaf, potatoes, charlotte potatoes, swiss chard, rainbow chard, rhubarb chard, pak choi, mizuna, apples, pears, swede, parsnips, romanesco, savoy cabbage, january king cabbage, sprouts.

DECEMBER: sprouts, sprouting brocolli, romanesco, curly kale, Russian red kale, swiss chard, rainbow chard, rainbow chard, squashes, parsnips, swedes, pursalanne, january king, savoy cabbage, leeks, pak choi, mizuna, rosemary, thyme, parsley, sage, bay leaf, apples, pears

Squash & Lentil Soup

Serves 4-6

1 tbsp olive oil
500g/1lb 4oz diced squash (Butternut, Kabocha or Crown Prince
  are good for this)
1 medium onion, finely chopped
2 cloves garlic, finely sliced
1 tsp ground cumin
1 tbsp tomato purée
1 litre/2 pints water or vegetable stock.
100g/4oz red lentils
Salt and black pepper

Heat the olive oil in a suitable pan.

Add the squash and onions and coat with the oil. Cook gently over a low-medium heat for about 10 minutes, this will slightly caramelise the squash.

Add the garlic and ground cumin, stir and cook for about 3–4 minutes.

Add the tomato paste, water or stock, lentils and the seasoning. Bring to the boil and then simmer gently for about 25 minutes or until the squash is soft and the lentils cooked.

Pour into a liquidiser and blend until smooth.

Leek & Potato Soup

Serves 6

When you buy the leeks for this, make sure you buy a whole one and not one that is trimmed. What is that all about? After all, indirectly you are really paying for it. Trimmed leeks in nice little packs – yuk! The green part not only adds more depth of flavour, but contributes to a nice green colour. At its best, a great simple soup, at worst grey sludge springs to mind!

Knob of butter
1 medium, finely chopped onion
2 cloves garlic, finely sliced
1 large leek, green and all (400g/1lb approx), finely sliced and washed
400g/1lb diced potato
1.2 litres/2 pints vegetable stock or water
Salt and freshly ground black pepper
A little double cream (optional)

Heat the butter in a suitable saucepan.

Add the onions and cook gently with a lid for 5 minutes with no colour.

Add the garlic and sliced leeks, stir well with the onions, season with a little salt and pepper. Place the lid back on and cook gently for about 5 minutes, or until the leeks have slightly softened.

Add the potato and hot stock. Bring to the boil and then simmer gently for about 20 minutes or until the potatoes are cooked.

Pour into a food liquidiser and blend until smooth. Add cream if you wish.

Parsnip, Apple & Curry Soup

Serves 4–6

Good knob of butter
1 medium onion, finely chopped
500g/1lb 4oz parsnips, peeled and chopped
1 clove garlic, thinly sliced
1 tsp medium curry powder
100g/4oz diced potato
200g/8oz diced bramley apple or other suitable cooking apple
1 litre/2 pints of water or vegetable stock
Salt and black pepper
2tbsp double cream (optional)

Heat the butter in a suitable saucepan. Add the onion and sweat in the butter until softened. Add the parsnips, garlic and the curry powder and stir well. Cook over a medium heat for about 5 minutes.

Add the potato, apple, water and seasoning. Bring to the boil and simmer gently for about 30 minues or until all the vegetables are soft.

Pour into a liquidiser and blend until smooth. Add the cream if you wish.

Pointed Cabbage & Dry Cured Bacon

Serves 4

Simple and delicious, a regular feature every Christmas at Walker base camp. This is quick and easy, so can be left to the last minute.

40g/1 $1/_2$oz butter
1 pointed cabbage
4 rashers dry cured bacon
Medium sized onion, finely sliced
Salt and pepper

Take the pointed cabbage and cut it into four, wash it well, then shred the cabbage as fine as you can. Cut the rashers of dry cured bacon into small strips and place in a frying pan and cook over a medium heat with a knob of butter until a little crispy.

Add the finely sliced onion and the remaining butter and sauté until soft. Add the cabbage to the pan and mix well, season with a little salt and black pepper.

Cook over a medium heat for about 5 minutes – the cabbage should have a slight bite when cooked.

Baked Leeks & Blue Cheese

Serves 4

1kg/2lb 8oz leeks
100ml/4fl oz double cream
50g/2oz Gorau Glas cheese
Salt and black pepper
Handful of coarse breadcrumbs

Trim the leeks and then depending on the length cut them into 2–3 pieces. Wash them well in some salty water.

Cook the leeks in boiling salted water for 5 minutes. Drain well and place in a baking dish.

Boil the double cream and whisk in the blue cheese until it is melted. Season with salt and pepper and pour over the leeks. Cover with tin foil and then bake in the oven at 180°C/375°F, gas mark 5 for 30 minutes.

Remove the foil and sprinkle over some breadcrumbs and return to the oven for 10 minutes, until the crumbs are brown and a little crisp.

Braised Onions

Serves 4

4 medium onions, cut in half
25g/1oz butter
100ml/4fl oz red wine vinegar
100ml/4fl oz red wine
1 small sprig rosemary
1 dessert spoon of white sugar
Salt and black pepper

Heat a suitable frying pan or flameproof oven dish and add the butter. Place the onions in flat side down and cook over a gentle heat for 15 minutes, or until nice and golden brown.

If you want to cook them on top of the stove, add the red wine vinegar, red wine, sugar, rosemary and seasoning. Cover with a lid or tin foil and then cook very gently for about 1 hour. When the onions are ready, the liquor should have reduced sufficiently to glaze the onions.

You can also cook these in the oven, just transfer the browned onions to a dish and proceed to add the remaining ingredients. Cover with a lid or tin foil and cook in the oven at 180ºC/375ºF, gas mark 4 for about an hour.

Carrots & Mint

Serves 4

450g/1lb 2oz carrots
50ml/2fl oz water
15g/³/₄oz butter
Salt and black pepper
Dessert spoon of chopped mint leaves

Peel and thinly slice the carrots.

Place in a saucepan with the water, butter and salt and pepper. Cover with a cartouche (round piece of greaseproof paper) and place on a medium heat.

Bring to the boil and simmer until the carrots are cooked with a slight bite and the liquid has evaporated.

Add the chopped mint leaves.

Roast Parsnips

Serves 4

A classic, rightly so and still the best way to eat parsnips. Parsnips vary greatly in size, so the cooking time will depend a lot on that.

700g parsnips/1lb 12oz parsnips
25g/1oz butter
1 tbsp vegetable oil
Salt and black pepper
1 good tbsp honey

Peel the parsnips and cut them into 3–4 pieces.

Heat a roasting tray with the butter and oil.

Put the parsnips in the pan and coat with the fat. Season with salt and pepper.

Cook in the oven at 190ºC/375ºF, gas mark 5 for about 30–40 minutes, turning them occasionally.

Add the honey with about 5 minutes of cooking left, coat the parsnips well.

Purple Sprouting Broccoli, Lemon & Olive Oil

Serves 4

Take 500g/1lb 4oz purple sprouting broccoli and trim any thick parts at the end.

Wash well and then cook then cook in a little boiling salted water for about 5–7 minutes. Drain well.

Whisk together juice of $^1/_2$ lemon and 50ml/2fl oz olive oil. Toss the broccoli in the oil and season with salt and black pepper.

Sprouts, Bacon & Shallots

Serves 4

Confession time... I'm not a great fan of the humble sprout, and I definitley wouldn't be fighting to take it to a desert island with me! Still, they are very good in bubble and squeak, and also in this combination. The sprouts are first boiled for about 8 minutes, then made cold and cut into quarters. Sprouts should never be *al-dente* but here they retain a little bite.

500g/1lb 4oz sprouts
3 rashers of dry cured streaky bacon, finely sliced
2 shallots, finely sliced
Good knob of butter
Salt and black pepper

Boil the sprouts in boiling salted water for about 8 minutes or until just tender. Drain and then refresh in iced water. When they are cold, cut them into quarters.

Heat a frying pan and add the bacon and fry until it is crispy. Add the butter and shallots and cook over a gentle heat until the shallots are soft.

Add the sprouts and seasoning, toss well together and cook for about 5 minutes over a medium heat, turning occasionally. They should be becoming a little softer but still retain a slight bite. You can always cook them a little more if you wish.

Russian Red Kale, Garlic & Lemon

Serves 4

500g/1lb 4oz Russian red kale
2 cloves garlic, crushed
2 shallots, finely sliced
Good splash of olive oil
1 strip lemon zest

Gently sauté the shallots in the olive oil until soft, add the garlic and cook for a few minutes.

Add the kale, strip of lemon zest and salt and black pepper. Add a few tablespoons of water.

Cover with a lid and steam through for about 5 minutes.

Drain any excess liquid and serve.

Cheesy Potato & Swede

Serves 6–8

900g/2lb 4oz large diced potato
450g/1lb large diced swede
100g/4oz Snowdonia original cheese, grated
50g/2oz butter
Sea salt
Black pepper

Put the potatoes and swede in a suitable pan and add enough water to cover. Season with salt and place on the heat, bringing to the boil. Cover with a lid and simmer gently until tender.

Drain and shake gently to rough up the potatoes slightly.

Place into a baking dish and mix in the remaining ingredients.

Cover with foil and bake in the oven at 200ºC/400ºF, gas mark 6 for about 40 minutes. Remove the foil for the last 15 minutes to allow the cheese to brown a little.

Humble Cake

Serves 4

My second and final way to use the humble sprout is in this sort of bubble & squeak. You will need a good floury potato for this to give the best results.

1kg/2lb 8oz potatoes, Cara or King Edward are good
200g/8oz cooked sprouts
200g/8oz finely sliced onions, cooked in butter until soft
25g/1oz butter, melted
Salt and black pepper

Peel and cut the potatoes into even size pieces. Place in cold water, add a little salt and bring to the boil, and simmer gently until just cooked. Drain and mash.

Roughly chop the sprouts. Add them and the onions to the potato. Add the melted butter and seasoning. Mix well.

Shape them into small cakes.

Heat a heavy based black pan or non-stick pan. Add a little oil and butter. Dust the cakes lightly in flour and place in the pan. Cook over a medium heat until lightly brown on the base, turn them over and repeat.

Pistyll Pan Potatoes

Serves 4

One day I'm caught a little short of locally grown vegetables...
well, I had some potatoes and carrots. I had purchased 5 dozen
eggs in the morning from Hen-Dy-Eggs and a sack of potatoes
from their neighbours. You need to use a potato that will keep its
structure during cooking – King Edward, Maris Piper and Cara
are good. The eggs were collected that morning, so were ultra
fresh. This is a simple, comforting supper dish where the sliced,
layered potatoes are cooked with butter in an ovenproof pan.
Finished with cheese, bacon and eggs, and all in the same pan!

1 kg/2lb 8oz potatoes
50g/2oz butter
Sea salt and black pepper
8 rashers dry cured bacon
4 eggs
50g/2oz cheddar cheese, grated

Peel and thinly slice the potatoes. Place the butter in an
ovenproof, heavy based frying-type pan. Layer the potatoes in the
pan and season well with sea salt and black pepper. Place in a hot
oven, 200ºC/400ºF, gas mark 6 and cook for about 45 minutes.
Press the potatoes down firmly with a fish slice after about 20
minutes.

When the potatoes are ready, add the rashers of dry cured
bacon and return to the oven. Cook until the bacon is crispy.
Now crack four eggs into the pan and sprinkle with the cheddar
cheese (I actually used Snowdonia Original for this). Return to
the oven and cook until the white of the egg is just set, but the
yolk remains soft and runny.

Roast Potatoes

Everyone loves them, soft melting centres, crispy, crusty outside and a sprinkling of coarse sea salt. What's the secret of the humble roast spud, then? Firstly, the right potato variety is crucial. What you are looking for is a potato with a good dry matter. Some of the red potatoes are good — Desiree, Romano — also whites like Maris Piper, King Edwards, and I find Cara excellent. Cara is what I used in this recipe, again supplied by Joyce up on the hill. Looked after themselves pretty well, while I had a hot, steamy bath! Perfick!

Allow one large potato per person. Peel and cut each potato into four. Place in a pan of cold water and bring to the boil, simmering gently until the outside shows signs of breaking slightly.

Drain and shake around in the colander; this will rough up the edges to give the potatoes a nice crustiness. While the potatoes are simmering, place a roasting tray with a little vegetable oil in a hot oven at 220°C/425°F, gas mark 7.

When the oil is hot remove from the oven and add a generous amount of butter, roughly the same as the oil. Add the potatoes and coat well. Sprinkle over some sea salt and place back in the oven.

Cook for about 45 minutes, until golden and crispy.

NB: you may need to turn the potatoes from time to time to produce and even colour.

Potato & Artichoke Cake

Nothing to do with Jerusaleum and nothing to do with the globe artichoke. In fact it is a relative of the sunflower, native to Peru. Confused? You're not the only one! Whatever, they are really delicious and deserve a higher regard than they get.

There are several varieties of these tubers and they vary in colour from white, light tan, red or purple. They are small and knobbly, which makes them a little tricky to peel, but the effort is more than worth it. This a simple dish that benefits from the earthy nature of the artichokes. They also make one of the best soups I know with bacon.

600g/1lb 8oz potatoes
300g/12oz Jerusalem artichokes
50g/2oz butter, chopped
Sea salt
Freshly ground pepper

Peel the potatoes and artichokes. Slice them thinly and place them in a bowl. Season them well and then arrange them in an ovenproof dish. Top with the butter.

Place a piece of greaseproof paper over the top and bake in the oven at 190ºC/375ºF, gas mark 5 for about 45 minutes. Use a fish slice to press down after 20 minutes and then with 10 minutes to go.

Veggie & Blue Cheese Pasties

Serves 4–6

There seems to have been an explosion of pasty eating, which is great. They seem to be popping up in many large train stations in the country, and offer a delicious alternative to the normal rubbish that is offered by the burger chains.

Traditionally, the pastry is made with flour, lard and water, although in this recipe I'm using puff pastry. I apologise in advance to the Cornish community! Don't be shy with the pepper mill here, this gives the spice required to the end product. The blue cheese for this came from Margaret and Catrin Davies at Quirt Farm in Anglesey.

Puff pastry
100g/4oz finely sliced onion
100g/4oz chopped parsnip
150g/6oz chopped swede
300g/12oz chopped potato
50g/2oz chopped leek
Salt
Black pepper
100g/4oz Gorau Glas blue cheese
Beaten whole egg

In a bowl, mix all the vegetables together. Add some salt and plenty of black pepper.

Roll out the puff pastry. You can make these pasties whatever size you like, so choose a round plate that is suitable. Use the plate to cut the pastry to size. Add a generous amount of the vegetable mix and crumble over a little cheese.

Brush the edges with a little egg wash and then fold over the pastry. Press down and make sure it is sealed and then crimp the edges with your fingers.Repeat the process with the remaining vegetables and cheese.

Place them on a lightly greased baking tray and brush with some beaten egg.

Bake in an oven at 200ºC/400ºF, gas mark 6 for about 40 minutes.

Gorau Glas Soufflé

Serves 4

This might possibly be one of the most expensive cheese soufflé ever! Don't panic when making soufflés, they are quite straightforward if you follow a few rules. You can make individual ones or one large one, both will be very good.

Also, remember the golden rule – 'the soufflé comes to the people, not the people to the soufflé'.

50g/2oz butter
40g/1 1/2 oz plain flour
100ml/4fl oz double cream
200ml/8fl oz milk
1/2 tsp English mustard
90g/3 1/2oz blue Gorau Glas blue cheese
4 egg yolks
5 egg whites
Salt and black pepper

Start by heavily buttering your ramekins or a large soufflé dish. Place in the fridge and when set repeat the process.

Melt the butter in a saucepan and add the flour, mix well and cook gently for 2–3 minutes.

Mix the double cream with the milk.

Add the liquid a little at a time, allowing it to boil each time and beating until it is smooth. Add the remaining liquid and then remove from the heat and stir in the blue cheese. Whisk in the egg yolks.

Whisk the egg whites with a pinch of salt until they are stiff.

Add a large spoonful to the cheese mix and beat in well.

Add the remaining egg white and gently fold in to the mix, until all the egg white is incorporated.

Pour the mix into your prepared dish/dishes and then cook in the oven at 200ºC/400ºC, gas mark 6 for about 20 minutes, or until well risen and brown on top.

Serve immediately.

preserving

Sloes

On my walks along the cliffs of Aberdaron, along to Fishermens Cove, I discovered big bushes of dark blue berries, that after closer inspection I found to be sloes. This member of the plum family is the only indigenous member of that crew to the British Isles.

Sloes grow in a curious way, in that they could appear to be ready in August. The colour may look right, but don't be deceived – they have another few months to go. You can usually start picking them at the beginning of October, maybe slightly earlier if you are lucky. The bushes are really thorny, so I recommend a decent pair of gardening gloves and a little patience. The rewards are well worth the effort, though.

Whatever you do, don't attempt to eat these little babies raw... on second thoughts, have a go and you will see what I mean! They are extremely tart, to say the least, and for the cook they lend themselves well to jellies, jams and sauces to match up with duck, game and pork. They also make an outstanding ice cream, which I will give you a recipe for later.

They are naturally very high in pectin, so this will give you a greater yield when making jellies and jams. Of course, they are most famously used to make sloe gin.

If you don't pick your own, you may be fortunate to spot them in your local farmers' markets, or if not, ask for them anyway because they may well have some on their farm and pick them especially for you.

I have included a few recipes for using your haul of sloes. So get out there and track them down!

Sloe Jam

Slow Purée
1.4kg/3lbs sloes
1 litre/2 pints water

Place the sloes in a large pan and cover with the water. Bring to the boil and then simmer very gently until well stewed and soft. Pass or push through a coarse sieve.

To make the jam you will need 1.25kg/3lb 2oz granulated sugar for every litre/2 pints of juice. Place in a suitable preserving pan and place on the heat. Bring to the boil and cook rapidly.

Remove any scum from the surface and stir occasionally. Cook until the setting point is reached. You can test this by placing a small spoonful on a saucer, and if it wrinkles after 30 seconds, the setting point has been reached. You can also purchase a sugar thermometer, which will tell you the temperature it needs to have reached.

Pour into sterilised jars, cover with jam pot lids and then a screw top if you feel it necessary.

Strawberry & Vanilla Jam

1kg/2lb 8oz strawberries, topped and hulled
750g/1lb 14oz granulated sugar
Juice of 1 lemon
$^1/_2$ vanilla pod or tsp vanilla extract

Put the strawberries in a preserving pan and place on a high heat. Bring to the boil and then add the sugar, lemon juice and vanilla pod.

Boil rapidly for about 20–25 minutes, or until the setting point is reached.

You need to be careful with this jam towards the end of cooking, as it is prone to stick. So when you think it is nearly ready keep stirring.

Stir in a knob of butter.

Pour into sterilised jars.

Cover with a jam seal.

Gooseberry & Lavender Jam

1kg/2lb 8oz gooseberries
750ml water
750g/1lb 14oz granulated sugar
3–4 lavender flowers

Place the gooseberries and water in a preserving pan.

Bring to the boil and simmer gently for about 35–40 minutes until soft and pulpy.

Pass through a coarse strainer, be sure to get as much through as possible.

Add the sugar and the lavender flowers.

Place the pan back on the stove on a gentle heat. Stir to dissolve the sugar and then increase the heat.

Boil rapidly for about 20–25 minutes, or until the setting point is reached.

Pour into sterilised jars and seal.

Damson Jam

1kg/2lb 8oz damsons
750ml water
750g/1lb 14oz granulated sugar

Place the damsons and water in a preserving pan and bring to the boil.

Simmer gently for about 35–40 minutes or until soft and pulpy. Pass through a coarse sieve, be sure to push as much through as possible. Return the liquid to the pan and add the sugar.

Place back on the heat and on a low heat allow the sugar to dissolve and slowly bring to the boil.

Increase the heat and boil rapidly for about 35 minutes, or until setting point is reached.

Pour into sterilised jars and seal.

Ma's Raspberry Jam

My mum says this jam is the king of them all, so I've named it after her! It also happens to be the easiest and fastest of all the jams to make.

Place 1kg/2lb 8oz raspberries and 1kg/2lb 8oz of granulated sugar in a preserving pan.

Place on a gentle heat and dissolve the sugar and bring slowly to the boil.

Increase the heat and boil rapidly for about 20 minutes or until setting point is reached.

Add a small piece of butter to disperse any scum.

Pour into sterilised jar and seal.

Plain & Simple Blackcurrant Jam

1kg/2lb 8oz blackcurrant
750ml/1 ¹/₂ pints water
750g/1lb 14oz granulated sugar
Juice of 1 lemon

Place the blackcurrants in the preserving pan and add the water. Bring to the boil and then simmer gently for about 30 minutes or until the fruit is soft and pulpy.

Pass through a coarse sieve, be sure to push as much through as possible.

Pour back into the pan and add the sugar and the lemon juice.

Place on a low heat and stir to dissolve the sugar. Once this has happened, increase the heat and boil rapidly for about 20–25 minutes, or until setting point is reached.

Pour into sterilised jars and place on a jam seal.

Beetroot & Horseradish Chutney

A classic combination of earthy, sweet beetroot and the unique flavour and heat of horseradish. Try to use fresh horseradish, although this is very difficult to find, so buy a jar of plain minced horseradish from the shop.

1kg/2lb 8oz beetroot, peeled and coarsely grated
30g/1$^1/_2$ oz minced horseradish
500ml/20fl oz red wine vinegar
250g/10oz granulated sugar
1 sprig thyme
1 sprig rosemary
Small piece of bay leaf

Place all the ingredients in a preserving pan and place on a gentle heat.

Stir until the sugar has dissolved and then increase the heat. Bring to the boil and cook for about 35–40 minutes over a medium heat.

There should be a thick liquid that clings to the beetroot.

Spoon into sterilised jars and seal.

Red Onion Chutney

1kg/2lbs 8oz red onions
1 tbsp vegetable oil
2 cloves crushed garlic
$^1/_2$ tsp ground cinnamon
$^1/_2$ tsp ground cumin
250ml /10fl ozred wine vinegar
100g/4oz soft brown sugar

Cut the onions in half, remove the root and then cut in half again. Slice the onions very finely.

Heat the vegetable oil in a suitable pan and add the onions, coat with the oil and cover with a lid. Cook over a gentle heat for about 15 minutes until they have softened.

Add the garlic, cinnamon, cumin, red wine vinegar and the soft brown sugar.

Cover with a lid and then cook over a gentle heat for about 30 minutes. Remove the lid and cook for a further 20 minutes, or until most of the liquid has evaporated and the mixture is thick.

Place the chutney into sterilised jars and seal.

Pickled Cabbage & Carrots

I found myself with a lot of cabbage and carrots one day in March. Pickles are great because they keep for a long time and actually improve with age. You can pickle any vegetables you like and add different flavours like spices to add more character. I've kept this one quite simple, just flavouring with a little juniper and orange.

1 large white cabbage, weighing about 1kg/2.2lb
500g/1lb 4oz carrots
2 onions
2$^1/_2$ tbsps salt
500ml/1 pint cider vinegar
150ml/6fl oz water
8 juniper berries
2 strips of orange peel
6 peppercorns

Shred the cabbage really finely or use your food processor to grate it. Grate the carrots and finely slice the onions.

Place the vegetables in a large bowl and mix in 2 tbsps of the salt. Leave for 2 hours, to allow the vegetables to wilt.

Wash the vegetables thoroughly and drain well. Pack them into a large preserving jar, that has previously been sterilised.

Bring the cider vinegar, water, juniper berries, orange peel, peppercorns and the remaining salt to the boil.

Pour over the vegetables and then seal.

The pickle will be ready to eat in a week.

puddings

Building Walls

A question for you. You've been farming for many years, it's been in the family many more, things are a bit of a struggle right now. Then, one day someone comes to you and informs you that they will pay you three times as much an hour for rebuilding the traditional stone walls on your land. Beats collecting eggs for a living, or milking cows... and sleepless nights during lambing season.

This is the ludicrous scenario that William Jones and his family were faced with last year, when the Heritage Society approached them to do this very thing. William was obviously delighted with this massive boost to his income, hard work, yet well rewarded. Maybe he should give up farming altogether, get a normal nine-to-five job, even re-build walls on other farmers' properties? Paid holidays, pension, healthcare, sick pay, and sometimes much more. So why not?

Their farm in Pistyll near Nefyn affords dramatic views over Caernarfon Bay, and William spends many an hour admiring it while checking his cattle up on the hill. When I arrive, though, he is collecting eggs from some of his 700 hens. He and his wife diversified into raising chickens nine years ago, seeking to increase their income from the farm. To a point it has been successful, although it seems it is getting much tougher now. This year will perhaps be their last, a great disappointment to them both. However, they feel the odds are too stacked against them to continue. They will revert to just farming cattle and sheep, which is slightly more profitable than raising chickens.

Raising chickens is, they have found, very time consuming. They spend at least four or five hours a day with them, feeding, cleaning and collecting the eggs. Unlike in London where I live, there is not a great market for their eggs here, and the distances they travel to deliver them, for the money they receive, just isn't worth it. Oh, and William does the deliveries too. William also explains, they have found out they have not been getting access to the best feed and what they have been receiving is at vastly more expensive prices than the big boys. He says the same feed is available, it is just not advertised to them.

He used to sell at Bangor farmers' market, which happens every two weeks, and he persevered for a while, but again for the distance, the time it took out of his day and the small sales he made while there, it simply wasn't cost effective.

They had also thought about rearing chickens for eating, and looking at traditional breeds, something I thought would certainly be worthwhile. Again, though, and this is a theme throughout, where would they sell them? Who is going to pay £8–10 each for a chicken? There simply isn't the money in the area, and so they would again have to look further afield for a market.

Indeed, only the other day I was having a discussion with a chap who had reared chickens for years, and had only now decided to throw in the towel. He told me he could expect to receive £2 a kilo in these parts, but if he were nearer to London he might expect to make almost £6 a kilo.

William and his wife, like most people I have met in the area, are not scared of hard work. Indeed, many of them thrive on it – a fair deal is all they ask. In the summer months it is not uncommon for William to leave the house at 7am and not return until 10pm. They don't have the money to employ anyone either, which they confess would be a great help. It is very difficult because of the minimum wage, as people want a lot of money for doing very little and, most importantly, he only barely scrapes to the minimum wage himself! The minimum wage is in theory a great idea, and one that most people should support, but in these cases it seems a little tough to justify.

William asks me to join him up on the hill – he need to check his cattle. He likes it here, a peaceful place, and one where he can gather his thoughts. The views are truly amazing, and many miles of land and ocean stretch out in front of you.

There are many walls too, some in need of repair. Is this his next line of work? Despite everything, I feel it won't be, for William has a passion for the land and for farming. That connection is strong, and one that he will not relinquish.

Baked Custard Tart

Serves 10

Short crust pastry
150g/6oz plain flour
75g/3oz hard butter
Pinch salt
1 tsp sugar
Water

Filling
515ml/20fl oz double cream
125ml/5fl oz milk
2–3 tablespoons of honey
8 egg yolks
12 leaves lemon verbena

Make the pastry by rubbing the butter into the flour, salt and sugar, until it resembles fine breadcrumbs. Add enough water to bind into a smooth paste. Wrap in cling film and refrigerate for 30 minutes.

Pour the double cream, milk, honey and lemon verbena into a saucepan and bring to the boil. Remove from the heat and allow the lemon verbena to infuse for about 30 minutes.

Roll out the pastry and use to line a 20cm/8" flan case and bake blind in the oven at 220°C/425°F, gas mark 7 for 15 minutes. Remove the beans for the last 5 minutes to allow the base to colour slightly.

Whisk the egg yolks and pour over the warm milk, whisk thoroughly and return to the pan. Cook over a gentle heat, stirring all the time with a wooden spoon, until it coats the back of the spoon.

Pour into the pastry case and bake for about 20–25 minutes at 160°C/325°F, gas mark3, or until set and the top is glazed.

Lemon Verbena Ice Cream

In my opinion, lemon verbena is a herb that should receive much more attention from cooks. It belongs to the same family as Mexican Oregano, which certainly surprised me at the time. It has a heavenly fragrance, that packs a great lemony punch, and can substitute for lemon when a less acidic note is required.

600ml/24fl oz double cream
300ml/12fl oz milk
7 egg yolks
180g/7oz vanilla sugar or 180g caster sugar & few drops
  vanilla extract
Small handful of lemon verbena leaves

Put the double cream, milk and lemon verbena leaves in a saucepan and bring to the boil.

Remove from the heat and leave to one side for about $^1/_2$ hour, to allow the lemon verbena to infuse.

Whisk up the egg yolks with the vanilla sugar. Reheat the milk until it is very hot again. Pour over the eggs and whisk thoroughly. Put the mix back in the pan and cook over a gentle heat, stirring all the time with a wooden spoon.

When the mix thickly coats the back of the spoon, remove and allow to cool.

Place the mix in the refrigerator and chill.

Pour into the ice cream machine and churn.

Raspberry Meringue Ice Cream

Serves 4

600ml/24fl oz double cream
300ml/12fl oz milk
7 egg yolks
180g/7oz caster sugar
200ml/8fl oz puréed raspberries
2 soft quenelles, as for Aberdaron Mess (p. 209)

Boil the milk and cream.

Whisk together the egg yolks and caster sugar.

Whisk the boiling liquid into the eggs.

Return to the pan and cook over a gentle heat, stirring all the time, until it coats the back of a spoon. Allow to cool and then place in the fridge until well chilled.

Stir in the raspberry purée and then churn in the ice cream machine.

Towards the end of churning add some broken pieces of the meringue.

Sloe Ice Cream

500ml/20fl oz milk
500ml/20fl oz double cream
$^1/_2$ cinnamon stick
6 large egg yolks
350g/14oz caster sugar
250g/8oz sloe puree, as for sloe jam (p. 180)

Place the milk, cream and cinnamon stick in a saucepan.
Bring slowly to the boil.

In a separate bowl whisk the eggs with the sugar.

Pour the boiling milk and cream over the eggs and sugar and
whisk well.

Pour the mix back into the pan and cook over a very gentle heat,
stirring continuously with a wooden spoon.

The custard is ready when it coats the back of the spoon. Don't
ever allow the mixture to boil or it will curdle and split.

Remove from the heat. Allow to cool slightly and then stir in the
sloe puree.

Place in a container in the fridge.

When it is chilled, pour it into an ice cream machine and churn.

Tregwylan Pancakes

Serves 4

A rich, creamy, buttery pancake, a lot more sophisticated than your average version. They are quite delicate, so I don't recommend any flipping antics. I served a couple of these with the sautéed apples, brandy and honey and a good dollop of lightly whipped cream with an extra drizzle of heated honey.

55g/2oz melted butter
150ml/6fl oz double cream
200ml/8fl oz milk
80g/3oz plain flour
1 large egg
1 tsp caster sugar

Place the flour, egg and half the milk in a large bowl and whisk until thick and smooth. Add the remaining ingredients and whisk well.

Heat a suitable black pan or non-stick pan and rub with a little butter. Pour in a little of the pancake mix and immediately tilt the pan, so that the mixture spreads thinly and evenly.

Cook for about 1 minute over a medium heat and then carefully turn over. Cook for another 45 seconds and turn out onto a plate. Repeat with remaining mixture.

Serve as suggested or your own favourite way.

Apples, Honey & Brandy

Serves 4

700g/1lb 12oz eating apples (I used Fiesta)
25g/1oz butter
1 capful brandy
1 tsp fine lemon zest
2 tsps wildflower honey

Peel the apples, cut them into quarters and remove the core. Cut them into quite thick slices.

Heat the butter in a suitable wide frying pan. When the butter is hot and a little frothy, throw in the apples. Coat them in the butter.

Over a medium heat cook the apples, turning them occasionally, for about 4–5 minutes.

Add the brandy and flambé.

Add the lemon and honey. Stir into the apples and cook for a further minute.

Apple & Almond Tart

Serves 8

This is based on the classic speciality dessert of clafoutis from the Limousin region of central France. Traditionally, it would always have contained cherries and was not made with a pastry. You will usually see this more as a tart these days. I have added ground almonds to the recipe, which are excellent with the apples and light egg and cream batter. This is also very good with pears, plums, damsons and of course lovely juicy cherries.

Pastry (as for Apple & Bulace Tart, p. 201)

Batter
2 large eggs
4oz/100g granulated sugar
2oz/50g ground almonds
100ml /4fl oz double cream
100ml/4fl oz milk
Few drops vanilla extract

Use the pastry to line a 20cm/8" loose bottom pastry case. Bake this blind.

Peel, core and slice 700g/1lb 12oz mixed apples (Bramleys, Coxes, Spartan, Russet, Jonagold, etc.) thickly and place in the case.

Whisk up all the ingredients for the batter. Pour over the apples.

Bake at gas 200ºC/400ºF, gas mark 6 for about 45–50 minutes or until set. Allow to cool, best served slightly warm.

Apple & Bulace Tart

Serves 8

The bulace tree bears a fruit not dissimilar to the damson, yet a little sweeter and with a round stone inside, not oval. I kept hearing about these from the locals and was determined to find some. Many farmers planted these years ago as a source of fruit for themselves, and that is where you will find them. If you're lucky, they may be hanging over the edge of fields in the road. I was fortunate enough to gather mine while at Elwyn's in Rhyd-y-Cladfy. He had many trees around a pond near where he raises his poultry, and was only too glad to let me have as many as I wanted. He confessed to being fed up with them!

This recipe makes a rich, dark tart, and is delicious served with vanilla ice cream, real custard or lashings of good cream. You can make this recipe with damsons as well.

Pastry
200g/8oz plain flour
100g/4oz local butter, chopped
1 egg
50g/2oz sugar
Pinch salt

Rub together the flour and butter until they resemble breadcrumbs. Pour onto the work surface and make a well. Whisk up the egg, sugar and salt in a bowl. Pour into the well and gradually incorporate with your hand, being careful not to break the ring. Mix well together to form a dough. Wrap in cling film or greaseproof paper and place in the fridge for 20 minutes.

Filling
450g/1lb cooking apples, peeled, quartered and sliced
300g/12oz bulace purée

150g/6oz granulated sugar
1 cinnamon stick
100g/4oz fried fresh breadcrumbs

Roll out two-thirds of the pastry and use to line a 20cm/8" loose bottomed cake tin.

Mix the bulace purée with 100g/4oz of the sugar and breadcrumbs. Place a layer of thick plum mixture in the base. Scatter in apple slices and the remaining granulated sugar. Add the cinnamon stick, and top with the remaining bulace mixture.

Roll out the remaining pastry and use to cover the top. Pinch down the edges and cut off any excess pastry.

Bake at 220°C/425°F, gas mark 7 for 10 minutes, then reduce the heat to 200°C/400°F, gas mark 6 for about 30 minutes.

Remove from the oven and allow to cool slightly. Remove from the tin and serve warm.

Apple Pie

Serves 8

I've used four different varieties of apples in this recipe. It might seem like a bit of hassle, but when you taste it, you will understand. The contrast in textures, flavour, sweetness and tartness gives this an extra edge. It makes the simple seem dramatic and it tastes incredible.

Pastry (as for Apple & Bulace Tart, p. 201)
1kg/2lb 8oz of mixed apples, Bramleys, Russet, Spartan and Coxes, peeled, quartered and thickly sliced
50g/2oz unsalted butter
100g/4oz muscovado or soft brown sugar
$^1/_2$ tsp ground cinnamon
50g/2oz breadcrumbs, fried in a little butter

Roll out two-thirds of the pastry and use to line a 20cm/8" medium loose bottomed cake tin.

Place butter and sugar in a large frying pan. Melt gently to incorporate together. Stir in the apples and coat with sugar mix and cook over a medium heat for 2–3 minutes. Add the breadcrumbs and cinnamon. Allow to cool slightly.

Spoon into the lined pastry case. Roll out remaining pastry and place over the top. Crimp down the edges and cut off excess pastry. Brush with a little beaten egg white and sprinkle generously with granulated sugar.

Bake for 40 minutes at 200ºC/400ºF, gas mark 6 until pastry is golden.

Apple Sorbet

1kg/2lb 8oz apples, Bramleys or other sharper apples
200ml/8fl oz water
200g/8oz granulated sugar
Juice of $1/2$ lemon

Peel, quarter and core the apples. Slice the apples and put them in a suitable pan to cook. Add the water and sugar. Place on the heat and stir until the sugar is dissolved.

Place on a lid and cook gently for about 20 minutes or until all the apple is soft.

Pour into a liquidiser and blend until smooth. Alternatively, you can push it all through a sieve.

Stir in the lemon juice, place in a bowl and chill.

Place it in an ice cream maker and churn until ready.

Apple & Blackcurrant Jelly

Serves 4

Jelly is one of those fun things we all remember from our childhood. Well, I'm not sure about you, but I'm still a sucker for it. Incredibly easy to make, you can adapt it with many different flavours. I used some of Hooton's Fiesta apple juice for this, and it produced a great result. The beauty of choosing a single variety apple juice is that you can have the character you want. If you would like your jelly sharper, choose an apple variety that is a cooker.

400ml/16fl oz apple juice
75g/3oz blackcurrants
50g/2oz sugar
3 leaves gelatine, soaked in water

Put the apple juice, blackcurrants and sugar in a saucepan. Simmer gently until the blackcurrants are soft. Pass through a fine sieve and pour back in the pan.

With the pan off the heat, whisk in the gelatine.

Pour into 4 separate glass dishes, or one larger one. Allow to cool, then place in the fridge to set.

Carrot Cake

Back in the 18th century it was commonplace to use root vegetables to flavour cakes and puddings. Beetroot, parsnips and carrots were favourite due to their natural sweetness. The best carrot cake I have ever eaten was at Glastonbury Festival in 1999. While spending some relaxing time wandering around the Green Field, I came across a stall that was selling delicious cakes and other sweet goodies. Actually, it was that good I went back for seconds! Never did get the recipe, though this one is a close reminder of it for me. Their version didn't have an icing for the top, so I've adopted the same approach.

225g/9oz butter
225g/9oz light muscovado cane sugar
4 eggs separated
Finely grated rind of $^1/_2$ orange
Juice of $^1/_2$ lemon
175g/7oz plain flour
3 tsps baking powder
50g/2oz ground almonds
100g/4oz chopped walnuts
350g/14oz carrots, peeled and finely grated
$^1/_2$ tsp mixed spice

Grease and line a deep 20cm/8" round cake tin.

Cream the butter and sugar together until light and fluffy. Beat in the egg yolks until well mixed. Add the orange zest, lemon juice, flour, baking powder, mixed spice, ground almonds and chopped walnuts. Beat these well into the mix.

Whisk up the egg whites in a clean bowl, until they offer stiff peaks.

Add the carrots to the main mix and then half of the egg white. Beat them into the main mix.

Gently fold in the remaining egg white.

Place the mix in the prepared cake tin and bake in the oven at 180ºC/350ºF, gas mark 4 for about 1 hour 20 minutes. If it is colouring too quickily, simply cover it with foil.

Leave to cool slightly and then remove the cake onto a cooling wire.

Aberdaron Mess

Based on the classic 'Eton Mess', this is a version of a soft baked meringue, crushed raspberries and vanilla flavoured custard. If you don't want to make custard, some whipped cream would be equally good.

6 egg whites
2 egg yolks
150g/6oz caster sugar
200g/8oz fresh raspberries
150ml/6fl oz milk and cream
150ml/6fl oz double cream
vanilla extract

Place the egg whites in your bowl for the mixing machine. Add 10g/$^1/_2$ oz sugar and whisk on a medium speed until you have full, firm peaks. Fold in a further 90g/3$^1/_2$ oz caster sugar.

Lightly grease a baking sheet and cover with a sheet of greaseproof paper. Using 2 tablespoons, shape the meringue into rugby ball shapes, known as quenelles. Place in a cool oven 130°C/250°F, gas mark $^1/_2$ for about 2 hours.

For the custard, bring the milk and double cream to the boil. Add a few drops of vanilla extract. Whisk up the egg yolks with 50g/2oz caster sugar and pour over the boiling liquid. Whisk well and return to the pan and cook over a very low heat, stirring continuously until the mixture coats the back of a spoon. Allow to cool and refrigerate.

Crush up the raspberries. Serve one meringue with some raspberries and a spoonful of the custard.

Raspberry & Blackberry Tart

Serves 8

Raspberries are perhaps the king of all the soft fruits. At their best they are highly perfumed. They can be quite expensive, but balance this with the blackberries that you can scavenge from the hedgerows and you have a great fresh, vibrant tart that proves more economical than you first imagined.

1 recipe sweet pastry (p. 201).

Roll out the pastry and use to line a 20cm/8" loose bottomed flan tin. Dock the bottom with a fork. Then bake blind in the oven for about 10 minutes on 220°C/425°F, gas mark 7. Remove the beans for the last 3 minutes to allow the base to lightly colour. Leave to cool.

Meanwhile pour a 227ml/9fl oz tub of buttermilk and 400ml/16fl oz double cream into a suitable saucepan. Add half a cinnamon stick. Place on the heat and slowly bring it to the boil.

In a bowl crack 3 medium eggs and 1 egg yolk, whisk in 25g/1oz plain flour and 75g/3oz caster sugar. Gradually pour the hot cream mix onto the eggs, whisking all the time. Whisk well and return to the pan.

Place it back on a low heat and stir continuously with a wooden spoon, until the mixture thickly coats the back of the spoon. Pour the mix straight into the baked pastry case.

Allow to cool and go cold.

Scatter over 200g/8oz fresh raspberries and 200g/8oz fresh blackberries.

Raspberries in Lemon Verbena

Serves 4

I discovered this combination whilst playing around one day and hey presto, a match made in heaven.

250g/10oz fresh raspberries
125ml/5fl oz water
100g/4oz sugar
Drop of vanilla extract
4 leaves of lemon verbena

Place the water, sugar, vanilla essence and the lemon verbena in a saucepan. Place on a gentle heat and stir until the sugar has dissolved.

Bring to the boil and then remove from the heat immediately. Allow to cool and then refrigerate.

Add the raspberries and immerse in the syrup.

Serve with cream, ice cream, yoghurt or even some cocktails.

Poached Rhubarb in Elderflowers

Serves 4–6

This is a stunningly simple match-made-in-heaven kind of thing.
You can pick the elderflowers off the trees in June and then
freeze lots for use at a later date. This recipe uses the outside,
hardy rhubarb, and when I sell this on my stall I get Champagne
rhubarb from Peter Clarke of Kingcup Farm – it really is the best,
and gives a lovely pinky/red liquid at the end. In January and
February you can of course use the forced rhubarb which comes
mainly from Yorkshire, but I would recommend that you bring the
syrup to the boil and drop the rhubarb in, and then remove
immediately as it is far more delicate. The low heat of the oven
cooks this nice and gently, so the rhubarb keeps it shape and with
a slight bite. Serve this with cream, ice cream or yoghurt.

250g/10oz granulated sugar
1 tbsp elderflowers
500g/1lb 4oz rhubarb, chopped

Place the granulated sugar in an ovenproof pan, add a the
elderflowers and 50ml/2fl oz water. Bring slowly to the boil to
dissolve the sugar.

Add the chunks of rhubarb. Cover with a lid or tin foil.
Place in an oven at 150ºC/300ºF, gas mark 2 for about 35–40
minutes.

Remove from oven and allow to cool.

This will store in the fridge for a week and will actually improve a
little.

Thirty Mile Blackcurrant Pudding

Serves 8

I'd stocked up on some frozen berries from Hooton's and one day had an urge to make a baked cheesecake. I usually use curd cheese to make the mix, but I didn't come across any on my travels, so I decided to adapt the recipe using a little of Anne Parry's Caerphilly goats cheese. I thought the combination of sharp blackcurrants, cream and a hint of the cheese would work quite well.

I like quite a sharp taste with this recipe – if you prefer it a little sweeter, add a little more sugar to the filling.

Base
60g/2¹/₂ oz butter
25g/1oz caster sugar
¹/₂ egg, beaten
100g/4oz plain flour
25g/1oz crushed digestive biscuits

Cream the butter and sugar until light and fluffy.

Beat in the egg, flour and the crushed digestive biscuits. Mix well and then place into a 20cm/8" loose bottomed flan dish or spring form cake tin. Push in with your fingers until evenly distributed.

Filling
100g/4oz caster sugar
50g/2oz butter
2 eggs, beaten
25g/1oz plain flour
Zest and juice of 1 lemon
25g/1oz Caerphilly goats cheese

250ml/10fl oz double cream
200g/8oz blackcurrants, top and tailed

Cream the sugar and butter until light and fluffy.

Add the eggs and flour and beat well until smooth. Add the lemon zest and juice, then using a whisk mix in the cheese and double cream. Add a little to begin with to keep the mixture smooth.

Fold in the blackcurrants and pour the mix onto the base.

Bake for 35–40 minutes at 190ºC/ 375ºF, gas mark 5. It should be nice and brown when it is ready.

Allow to cool, then remove from ring.

Serve at room temperature.

Gooseberry Fool

Serves 4

300g/12oz gooseberries
50g/2oz caster sugar
250ml/10 fl oz double cream, lightly whipped
A few drops of vanilla extract

Top and tail the gooseberries. Then place them in a saucepan and add the sugar, cover with a lid and gently cook for about 5–10 minutes.

When the fruit is softened, remove from the pan and crush with a fork. Allow to cool.

Mix the crushed gooseberries with the whipped cream and the vanilla extract.

Chill in the fridge before serving.

Larkin's Rice Pudding

Serves 4–6

Rice pudding…yuk!! Some people only remember this from their school days and refuse to go near it. I started selling this at Marylebone Farmers' Market, and it got a resounding thumbs-up… I even managed to convert a few people.

To me rice pudding is a thing of magic and mystery. When you see the amount of rice to liquid at the beginning, you think this can't be right. Gradually, the rice absorbs the cream and milk and becomes really creamy, and with just a slight bite, flavours of cinnamon, vanilla, orange and lemon, the rounded flavour is a taste sensation. Never be scared again!

300ml/12fl oz full cream milk
150ml/6 fl oz double cream
A few drops of vanilla extract
fingernail sized piece of cinnamon stick
60g/1 1/4oz pudding rice
fingernail sized pieces of orange and lemon peel

Place the full cream milk and the double cream in a saucepan. Add the vanilla extract, cinnamon stick and lemon and orange peel. Bring to the boil.

Add the rice and reduce the heat so the liquid is just breaking the surface. Be sure to stir this every 10 minutes to prevent the rice sticking together.

Test the rice by eating a small piece – when ready it should have a slight bite. Remove from the heat and allow to cool. Stir it occasionally. Best served at room temperature.

Welsh Rabbit

Surely I've not got the right spelling for this, shouldn't it be rarebit? Well, it seems that the term 'rarebit' came 60 years after the original name for this dish. Originally, this was just simply cheese on toast. However, the addition of mustard was considered a good touch improve it. These days, we like a far richer version, and add beer, Worcestershire sauce and egg yolks. You need top quality cheese for this, otherwise the result will be very greasy.

I used two cheeses from Anne Parry's goats cheese range, and the beer was from Anglesey. I mixed the Double Gloucster and Caerphilly and produced a rich, goaty topping for my toast.

100g/4oz Anne's Double Gloucester, grated
100g/4oz Anne's Caerphilly, grated
25ml/1fl oz beer
25ml/1fl oz milk
1 tsp English mustard
2 egg yolks
Good splash of Worcestershire sauce

Heat the beer and milk in a small pan. Add the grated cheese, mustard and Worcestershire sauce and cook over a low heat, stirring with a wooden spoon until all the cheese is melted.

Remove from the heat and beat in the egg yolks.

Leave to cool and go cold.

Toast some slices of bread, spread with the cheese mix and then place under a hot grill to brown.

food directory

Here follows a list of food outlets that I found and used on my travels. I know there are many more people doing fantastic work in food in the area, so I can only apologise for not finding or visiting you.

Beef Direct

Contacts:	Brian & Fiona Thomas
Tel:	01248 470387
Web:	www.beefdirect.net
	Plas Coedana, Llannerch-y-medd, Anglesey LL71 8AA

Suppliers of organic pure bred Welsh black beef, Welsh Mountain lamb and pork.

Sell at farmers' markets in Manchester, Liverpool, New Ferry (Wirral), Altrincham, Wrexham, Ashton-under-Lyne. Mail order and some farm visits allowed by prior arrangement.

Tryfan Organics

Contact:	Gwyn Thomas
Tel:	01248 600400
	Blaen y Nant, Bethesda

Suppliers of organic Welsh Mountain lamb, pure bred Welsh black beef. Sells directly from home or mail order.

Also has a nature trail during the season (April–September).

Fferm Ty Isaf

Contact: Bini Jones
Tel: 01766 762608
Ffestiniog LL41 4LS

Supplier of organic full bred Welsh black beef and Welsh Mountain lamb. Sells by mail order.

Llechwedd Meats

Contact: Norman Roberts
Tel: 01248 422073
Gaerwen, Anglesey

Suppliers of organic Welsh black beef from Snowdonia farms and own Anglesey farm.

Anglesey Sea Salt

Contact: Mr David Lea-Wilson
Tel: 01248 430871
Web: www.seasalt.co.uk
Brynsiencyn, Anglesey LL61 6 TQ

Suppliers of Halen Mon a natural sea salt and Britain's only organically certified sea salt.

Deri Mon Smokery

Contact: David
Tel: 01248 410536
Web: derimon.freewebspace.com
Deri Isaf, Dulas Bay, Anglesey LL79 0DX

Farm shop, farmers' markets, mail order and in selected local stores. Suppliers of smoked fish and meats, game

Hen-dy-Eggs

Contact: William Jones
Tel: 01758 720610
Pistyll, Pwllheli, Gwynedd LL53 6LP

Suppliers of free range eggs, lamb and beef.

Hooton's Homegrown
Contact: Michael & Rosalind Hooton
Tel: 01248 430344
Web: www.hootonshomegrown.com
             Gwydryn Hir, Brynsiencyn, Anglesey

Farm shop supplying wide range of seasonal produce, meat, game, poultry and preserves, almost all of which is produced by them.

Peter Haywood
Contact: Peter Haywood
Tel: 01758 721349
             Edern

Honey producer and inspector

Brett Garner
Contact: Brett Garner
Tel: 01758 780420
             Rhiw

Supplier of pheasants and grey legged partridge.

Menna Jones
Contact: Menna Jones
Tel: 01758 780269

Supplies local crab, lobster and fish from their home in Aberdaron.

Lewis Jones
Contact: Lewis Jones
Tel: 01758 720154

Supplied me with oak chippings for smoking.

Llangybi Organics
Contact: Jill & Mike Langley
Tel: 01766 810915
             Ty'n Lon Uchaf, Llangybi, Pwllheli LL53 6LX

Supplier of organic vegetables. Box scheme only.

Menai Oysters
Contact: Shaun Krijnen
Tel: 01248 430878
              Dwyran, Anglesey

Supplies oysters and mussels. Mainly wholesale, but also sells at source.

Gallet-y-Beren Farm
Contact: Anne Parry
Tel: 01758 740233
              Gallet-y-Beren Farm, Rhyd-y-Cladfy

Supplier of goats and cows cheese. Available from farmers' markets and from source.

Quirt Farm
Contact: Margaret Davies
Tel: 01248 430570
              Dwyran, Anglesey LL61 6BZ

Supplier of Gorau Glas, an award winning soft blue cheese.

Selective Seafoods
Contact: Mary & Gareth White
Tel: 01758 770397

Supplier of crabs, lobsters, fish and other related products. Available from farm shop premises. Takes shellfish from Steve Harrison, who fishes out of Aberdaron and Sion Jenkins, who fishes out of Porth Colman.

South Caernarfon Creameries Ltd
Tel: 01766 810 251
              Rhydygwystl, Chwilog, Pwllheli,
              Gwynedd LL53 6SB

A farmer owned co-operative suppling milk, cream, cheese and buttermilk.

Herbs From Wales

Contact: Rowena & Phillip Mansfield
Tel: 01248 470231
             Carmel, Llanerchymedd, Anglesey LL71 7DD

Supplier of herbs for culinary and medicinal use. On site or mail order.

E.T. Jones

Contact: Ifan Jones
Tel: 01407 740257
             Bodedern, Anglesey

Traditional butcher, abattoir on site and supplies restaurants.

D & A Ellis and Son

Tel: 01248 852200
             Tryfan, Coastal Road, Benllech, Tyn-Y-Gongl,
             Anglesey LL74 8TR

Traditional butcher stocking locally reared meats, homemade pies, sausages and bacon.

Glasfryn Parc Farm Shop

Tel: 01766 810202
             4 miles east of Pwllheli, on A499 towards Carnarfon

Produces own beef, lamb and game in season. Stocks locally produced foods where possible.

Bwydlyn

Tel: 01758 612136
             19 Gaol Street, Pwllheli, Gwynedd LL53 5DB

Traditional butchers, stocking locally reared meats, curing own bacon and sausages.

Joyce & Emlyn

On the hill in Aberdarron. Suppling locals with vegetables and soft fruits during season.

Elwyn
Rhyd-y-Cladfy

Generally produces chickens, ducks, geese and turkeys for local people who know him. Stocks a few rare breed chickens.

Mary Gaunt
Penhwnllys Plas, Llangoed, Anglesey Ll58 8PW

Rears tradionally bred Red Poll and Shetland cattle, Jacob, Soay and Black Welsh Mountain sheep and Saddleback and Tamworth pigs.

index